Ray Charles and the Birth of Soul

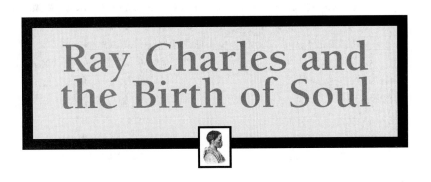

Other titles in this series:

A Dream Deferred: The Jim Crow Era

The Fight Renewed: The Civil Rights Movement

Forty Years of Medical Racism: The Tuskegee Experiments

The Harlem Renaissance

A History of Free Blacks in America

Marcus Garvey and the Back to Africa Movement

A Peculiar Institution: Slavery in the Plantation South

The Quest for Freedom: The Abolitionist Movement

Ray Charles and the Birth of Soul

Lucent Library of Black History

Adam Woog

LUCENT BOOKS

An imprint of Thomson Gale, a part of The Thomson Corporation

THOMSON
★
™
GALE

Detroit • New York • San Francisco • San Diego • New Haven, Conn.
Waterville, Maine • London • Munich

THOMSON

---*---

GALE

*This one's for Leah, who told me when she was little that she wanted to
play the saxophone "just like on the old Ray Charles records" . . .
and for Karen, who lets me play those old records almost as often as I like . . .
and for Paul Klein and Jeff Showman, for obvious reasons.*

LIBRARY OF CONGRESS CATALOGING-IN-PUBLICATION DATA

Woog, Adam, 1953–
    Ray Charles / by Adam Woog.
        p. cm. — (The Lucent library of Black history)
    Includes bibliographical references.
    ISBN 1-59018-844-6 (hardcover : alk. paper) 1. Charles, Ray, 1930–2004 2. Singers—United States—Biography. I. Title. II. Series.
ML420.C46W66 2005
782.42164'092—dc22

2005022586

Printed in the United States of America

Contents

Foreword   6

Introduction
The Genius of Soul   8

Chapter One
Early Childhood   13

Chapter Two
The School of the Road   26

Chapter Three
From Obscurity to Stardom   42

Chapter Four
The Genius   58

Chapter Five
A Rough Patch for the Genius   72

Chapter Six
The Elder Statesman of Soul   87

Notes   101
For Further Reading   104
Works Consulted   105
Index   107
Picture Credits   111
About the Author   112

Foreword

It has been more than five hundred years since Africans were first brought to the New World in shackles, and over 140 years since slavery was formally abolished in the United States. Over 50 years have passed since the fallacy of "separate but equal" was obliterated in the American courts, and some forty years since the watershed Civil Rights Act of 1965 guaranteed the rights and liberties of all Americans, especially those of color. Over time, these changes have become celebrated landmarks in American history. In the twenty-first century, African American men and women are politicians, judges, diplomats, professors, deans, doctors, artists, athletes, business owners, and home owners. For many, the scars of the past have melted away in the opportunities that have been found in contemporary society. Observers such as Peter N. Kirsanow, who sits on the U.S. Commission of Civil Rights, point to these accomplishments and conclude, "The growing black middle class may be viewed as proof that most of the civil rights battles have been won."

In spite of these legal victories, however, prejudice and inequality have persisted in American society. In 2003, African Americans comprised just 12 percent of the nation's population, yet accounted for 44 percent of its prison inmates and 24 percent of its poor. Racially motivated hate crimes continue to appear on the pages of major newspapers in many American cities. Furthermore, many African Americans still experience either overt or muted racism in their daily lives. A 1996 study undertaken by Professor Nancy Krieger of the Harvard School of Public Health, for example, found that 80 percent of the African American participants reported having experienced racial discrimination in one or more settings, including at work or school, applying for housing and medical care, from the police or in the courts, and on the street or in a public setting.

It is for these reasons that many believe the struggle for racial equality and justice is far from over. These episodes of discrimination threaten to shatter the illusion that America has completely overcome its racist past, causing many black Americans to become increasingly frustrated and confused. Scholar and writer Ellis Cose has described this splintered state in the following way: "I have done everything I was supposed to do. I have stayed out of trouble with the law, gone to the right schools, and worked myself nearly to death. What more do they want? Why in God's name won't they accept me as a full human being?" For Cose and others, the struggle for equality and justice has yet to be fully achieved.

In many subtle yet important ways the traumatic experiences of slavery and segregation continue to inform the way race is discussed and experienced in the twenty-first century. Indeed, it is possible that America will always grapple with the fallout from its distressing past. Ulric Haynes, dean of the Hofstra University School of Business has said, "Perhaps race will always matter, given the historical circumstances under which we came to this country." But studying this past and understanding how it contributes to present-day dialogues about race and history in America is a critical component of contemporary education. To this end, the Lucent Library of Black History offers a thorough look at the experiences that have shaped the black community and the American people as a whole. Annotated bibliographies provide readers with ideas for further research, while fully documented primary and secondary source quotations enhance the text. Each book in the series explores a different episode of black history; together they provide students with a wealth of information as well as launching points for further study and discussion.

Introduction

The Genius of Soul

There was music before Ray Charles, and there's music after Ray Charles. It's that stark a difference.

—SINGER BONNIE RAITT

In the 1960s, prominent African American comedian Flip Wilson performed a sketch in which he played Queen Isabella, the Renaissance-era ruler of Spain. In the skit, Isabella is preparing to fund Christopher Columbus's voyage to the New World in 1492. At the end of much comic speculation about what Columbus will find on his epic journey, the queen ecstatically shouts, *"Chris gon' find Ray Charles!"*[1]

Wilson's routine was funny, but his punch line made a serious point, acknowledging Ray Charles as a giant of American popular music and culture. Still in his thirties at the time, Charles was already internationally celebrated as the epitome of the American rags-to-riches story and the king of the uniquely American musical genres of rhythm and blues (R&B), and soul. Writing in the 1980s, jazz journalist Whitney Balliett summarized the singer's role when he stated that "Charles *is* the American Dream."[2]

Against All Odds

Charles epitomized this dream, in large part, because his life was a story of prevailing against extraordinary odds. Charles was by no means perfect; he had more than his share of problems, and he was a complex, difficult, and often contradictory person. Even Charles's worst flaws, however, were overshadowed by his accomplishments.

He was, first of all, a virtuoso musician. His gifts for singing and playing the piano alone would probably have assured him fame. But Charles was also a brilliant synthesizer of styles, radically melding different forms and boldly crossing uncrossed boundaries. Thanks to his innovations, Charles permanently changed the course of black music—and of American music altogether.

One of Charles's startling innovations was to merge the frank sexuality of the blues with the religious passion of gospel. (Sometimes this melding of styles was blatant. One of his song titles, for instance, was "This Little Girl of Mine," which directly borrows from the old gospel song "This Little Light of Mine.") Charles's combination of sacred and secular music outraged many listeners, who felt it was disrespectful to religion, but it delighted millions more.

Furthermore, Charles's music was a cornerstone of a powerful and influential style—soul music—that flowered in the 1960s.

"Don't Stop There"

———————————■———————————

For decades, Ray Charles was a dominant force in music, though his exact niche was always difficult to define. Writer Thomas Thompson, in his *Life* magazine profile "Music Soaring in a Darkened World," had this to say: "The best blues singer around? Of course, but don't stop there. He is also an unparalleled singer of jazz, of gospel, of ballads, even, unlikely enough, of country and western. . . . If he never sang a note, he would [still] be one of the great jazz pianists, ranging from the low-down to the ice-cold geometrics of the far out."

"He Is Always Surprising"

━━━━━━━━━━ ■ ━━━━━━━━━━

Jazz writer Whitney Balliett, in this passage from his book *American Singers: 27 Portraits in Song*, reflects on the remarkable versatility of Charles's voice:

> Charles can sing anything short of lieder [classical German art songs] and opera. He has recorded standard popular songs, country-and-Western music, downhome blues, American anthems such as "Old Man River" and "America," novelty numbers, rock and roll, the Beatles, and folk music. He works with equal ease in front of a small jazz band, a big band, vocal groups, choruses, and strings. . . . He can shape his baritone voice into dark, shouting blocks of sound, reduce it to a goose-pimpling whisper, sing in a pure falsetto, yodel, resemble Nat Cole at his creamiest, and growl and rasp. He is always surprising.

With his talent for the piano and his dynamic voice, Ray Charles established himself as one of the most popular musicians of the twentieth century.

Soul quickly became the dominant style of black popular music, and its enduring popularity spread around the world. In the years since, soul has also deeply affected mainstream musical styles, like rock and roll, as well as more recent black music, like funk and hip-hop.

Another of Charles's innovations was to explore white country-and-western music. Until Charles arrived, country music had not, for the most part, inspired black musicians. But Charles's pioneering interpretations, far from underscoring the differences between black and white music, clearly demonstrated the similarities. Charles's groundbreaking synthesis of these seemingly separate musical streams was a resounding success, both commercially and artistically.

In addition to his brilliance as a musician—which earned him the nickname "the Genius"—Charles was also a pioneering African American businessman. At a time when such accomplishments were still rare for a black person, he created a multi-million-dollar, multifaceted corporate empire that encompassed a record company, a recording studio, and more. And, in an era when it was financially ruinous for most musicians to maintain large traveling bands, the Ray Charles Orchestra remained a thriving concern.

Charles accomplished all this against crushingly bad odds. First, he was born into a desperately poor family. Then he lost his sight completely by the age of seven. He was orphaned and entirely on his own, a working professional, by his early teens. For years, he was also a drug addict. Finally, during the era in which he lived, racism targeted black Americans personally and professionally; Charles faced prejudice, risked violence, and struggled to establish himself as the civil rights movement took hold in America.

Entertainer, Artist, American

As his millions of fans know, Charles prevailed brilliantly over these obstacles. In large part, this was because of his spectacular gifts as a creative artist. But it was also because of a powerful strength of purpose instilled in him at an early age by his strong-willed mother. This determination gave Charles a sense of self-reliance that served him well all his life.

Charles's strength of will was always in the service of one thing: his music. Music was the spark in Ray Charles's life, the engine that kept him moving, his heart and blood and bone. He often said that it was as vital to him as breathing. He had other loves: Women, chess, good southern cooking, and, for several years, heroin all held his attention. But music remained his greatest and most constant love. To paraphrase Duke Ellington, another iconic American performer: music was his mistress.

Charles was that rarity, a great artist who was also a wildly successful entertainer. As an artist, he forged a union between previously distinct musical styles and was a founding father of soul music. As an entertainer, meanwhile, Charles was an American institution long before his death in 2004.

Before all that came to pass, however, there was the black neighborhood of a small town in the Florida panhandle. There was music in the air there—when a bar owner played a piano, when people put money in a jukebox to hear scratchy records, when a radio picked up faint, faraway sounds. This was the environment in which Ray Charles Robinson grew up.

Chapter One

Early Childhood

When I say we were poor, I'm spelling it with a capital P. . . .
We were on the bottom of the ladder looking up at every-
one else. Nothing below us 'cept the ground.

— RAY CHARLES ON HIS CHILDHOOD

Ray Charles grew up in a tightly defined world. His boyhood home was Greenville, Florida, but his world then was even smaller than that; RC, as he was called, rarely ventured outside Jellyroll, Greenville's black neighborhood. Strictly segregated from the white part of town, Jellyroll was a quiet, hot backwater of wooden shacks and dusty streets, pecan and chinaberry trees, live oaks and piney woods.

Greenville (which everyone called "Greensville") was economically poor, as was much of the Deep South. But then, times were tough everywhere in the 1930s, when RC was a boy. The hardships of the Great Depression were threatening to crush the entire country; millions of people were out of work, and entire families were starving. Almost everyone was poor, and RC's family was among the poorest of the poor.

RC Is Born

And yet RC's childhood was rich in other ways. For one thing, his extended family, though unconventional, was close. The linchpin of this family was RC's mother, Aretha.

She had been born Aretha Williams, but when she was still young she was adopted by a family friend, Margaret Robinson, and became Aretha (or Retha) Robinson. Margaret also had a grown son, Bailey, who worked as a mechanic and handyman for the railroad. Bailey's wife, Mary Jane, had a job at a local lumber mill.

Ray Charles grew up in a poor black neighborhood in Greenville, Florida, that consisted of dusty dirt roads lined with wooden shacks.

When the slender and good-looking Aretha was about fifteen, she became pregnant; Bailey Robinson was the father. To quiet the town's gossips, Aretha was sent to stay with relatives in Albany, Georgia. Her child, Ray Charles Robinson, was born there in the fall of 1930. No birth certificate survived, but he always celebrated his birthday on September 23.

Aretha returned to Greenville with her infant son; soon after that, Bailey and Mary Jane Robinson separated. Bailey then moved to another small Florida town and started a new family. He was rarely present in his son's life afterward.

The dominant person in RC's life instead was Aretha. She was not physically strong; in fact, according to some accounts, she sometimes used a cane. But she was determined to work hard at whatever jobs she could handle, such as taking in laundry or cleaning houses. Furthermore, although not formally educated beyond about the fifth grade, Aretha was intelligent, with a forceful personality and a steely will; RC's childhood playmate, Gertrude Riddick, recalled that "Retha was weak in body, but strong in mind."[3]

There was another powerful presence in RC's life. Mary Jane Robinson, the wife that Bailey left, remained close to Margaret and Aretha. She doted on Retha's boy and essentially became his second mother. He frequently stayed at her house overnight, and she always indulged him with treats; he recalled later that "she was constantly buying me baloney, weenies, and candy, the kind of food that Mama couldn't afford."[4]

"We Were Tough Kids Then"

Within a year of RC's birth, Aretha had another son, George. (It is unclear who George's father was.) As they grew up, the boys were inseparable. Together they did their daily chores, which included chopping wood for the fire and hauling water from a river, and every Sunday they attended the New Shiloh Baptist Church with the adults, singing and praying with the rest of the congregation.

But their lives were not exclusively work and church. The boys also had ample time for playing together, in the woods around Greenville and in its streets. Ray later recalled that he, his brother, and their friends were independent kids who learned early on to fend for themselves and find their own solutions to problems: "We were tough kids then, stuck in that little town in the woods in the South. . . . It was different from now and it helped you later in life. If we fell out of a tree and knocked our wind out, we got up and kept running. If we got cut, we'd stick some clay dirt in the cut, or a cobweb, and that would clot it."[5]

Both boys were bright; George was especially good at doing complicated math in his head. But RC's strong point, even from an early age, was music. Even then, the singer later recalled, music had the power to grab him fiercely: "I was a normal kid, mischievous and into everything, but I loved music; it was the only thing that could really get my attention."[6]

Mr. Pit

Fortunately for RC, Aretha was friendly with the owners of Mr. Pit's Red Wing Café, a restaurant-bar that doubled as a general store. Mr. Pit's was the center of social life in black Greenville. Wiley Pitman and his wife, affectionately known as Mr. Pit and Miz Georgia, owned the place; Aretha Robinson worked there part-time.

The centerpiece of Mr. Pit's was its piano, and Wiley Pitman, a large, genial man, was an accomplished performer. He played in a lively style called boogie-woogie, which had been popularized by such musicians as Albert Ammons, Pete Johnson, and Meade Lux Lewis. Influenced by both early jazz and the blues, boogie-woogie was characterized by virtuoso speeds, strong rhythms steadily pumped out in the left hand, and lively, improvised figures in the right hand.

Despite his skill at the piano, Mr. Pit never earned a reputation outside of Greenville. According to Ray Charles, however, he could easily have been a pro if he had not chosen to stay in his small-town home. RC once asserted, "Now you won't find Mr. Pit in any history of jazz, and the man's not in the Down Beat Hall of Fame. But, sweethearts, you can take my word for it: Mr. Pit could play some sure-enough boogie-woogie piano."[7]

The Piano and the Jukebox

Mr. Pit's was an irresistibly fascinating draw to RC. When the boy was not playing outside or doing his chores, he could usually be

In a still from the 2004 film *Ray*, Wiley Pitman, the owner of a café in Greenville, teaches the young Ray Charles to play a simple tune on the piano.

found listening to Mr. Pit playing the piano. RC was also eager to try playing himself whenever he could.

Pitman encouraged the boy's enthusiasm. He taught RC the fundamentals of boogie-woogie rhythms and the rudiments of the blues, with its infinite variations on a basic three-chord structure. Mr. Pit also let RC fool around by himself on the piano, picking out melodies and trying new rhythms. RC recalled years later: "When he played, I'd run in and listen. He must of taken note. He would let me sit on the piano bench next to him and bang on the keys. I didn't know nothing. He would tell me, 'Play it, play it. You're doing fine.' I'll always love that man for that."[8]

For RC, almost as good as the café's piano was its jukebox. Whenever a bar patron put a nickel in this machine, RC would press his ear to the speaker to listen as closely as possible to its scratchy 78-rpm recordings of blues and jazz. In this way, RC heard a wide variety of popular performers. They included rough but emotive blues singers like Big Joe Turner and Tampa Red, with their huge voices and jumping instrumental backups. He also heard big bands—the dominant jazz style of the period—including such classic groups as those of Fletcher Henderson, Count Basie, and Duke Ellington. These bands used sophisticated, exciting arrangements to make many instruments sound like one voice, sometimes elegant and sometimes—to use an expression of the times—just gut-bucket.

Thanks to radio, an increasingly popular form of entertainment in the 1930s, RC also heard more than African American blues and jazz. Programs like *The Grand Ole Opry*, the nation's premier country radio show, exposed RC to a variety of white popular music as well. Black or white, the boy loved every bit of this richly varied musical palette, and it gave him a lasting appreciation for diverse styles. As the singer later put it, "I ain't real narrow in my tastes."[9]

Two Tragedies

In part because of his exposure to music and his experience playing the piano at Mr. Pit's, Ray Charles later considered that his early childhood had been happy. However, when he was still young, this happy existence received two serious blows. The first,

Like Breath or Blood

———————■———————

Charles always asserted that his blindness had nothing to do with his musical ability—that music was a big part of his life before his blindness. He reflects on this in a passage from Guy Martin's *Esquire* magazine article "Blue Genius":

I lost my sight completely when I was about seven, but I was playin' music before I went blind, or at least I was tryin' to. And music was the only thing that would stop me in my tracks as a child. I don't care what I was doin'. If I'm outside playin' with the cats, you know, with the boys, out there in the mud, and if that Wiley Pitman would start playin' that piano, that would get my attention. So music is not somethin' I do on the side and I just happen to do it pretty good. Music is just as much a part of me as your breathin' or your bloodstream is to you. So they ain't no retiring from it; I'm gonna do it . . . till I die. This is all I know, and all I wanna know. And that's the truth. I don't think I'm good because I'm blind. I think I'm good because I'm good.

which occurred when RC was five, was the drowning death of his brother George.

George was fooling around in their mother's laundry tub one day, diving and laughing, when he slipped and went headfirst under the water. RC saw it happen and tried to pull his brother out, but he lacked the strength. By the time RC gave up and ran for help, it was too late: George was dead. It was RC's first real taste of tragedy, an event he remembered vividly all his life.

More misfortune came within months: RC began to lose his sight. The change was gradual, not sudden. He recalled, "It started by my eyes running like hell all the time. Not tears—it was too thick. It was more like mucus, and when I'd wake up in the morning it was so thick I'd have to pry my eyes open."[10]

Over time, the condition affected his eyesight. Painful pressure built up around the boy's eyes, and he increasingly had trouble seeing distinct shapes. Soon RC could make out only large forms, then only colors, then nothing more than day from night. By the age of seven, he was completely and irreversibly blind.

There were two doctors in Greenville, and only one, Dr. McCloud, was willing to see black patients. He did what he could for the boy, giving him eyedrops and advising him to avoid strong light. McCloud also sent Aretha and her son to a clinic in Madison, fourteen miles (22km) away—the greatest distance from home RC had traveled so far—but the doctors there were unable to help. No official diagnosis was ever made, but it is likely that the boy suffered from juvenile glaucoma, a rare condition that can lead to blindness if treatment is ineffective or unavailable.

Blind Does Not Equal Stupid

At first, the future seemed grim for RC. Begging, street-corner singing, and the simplest menial jobs were among the few options available for the typical blind person at the time. If that person was also African American, even less was expected.

It would thus have been easy for RC to lapse into helplessness and self-pity. However, Aretha Robinson refused to let her son

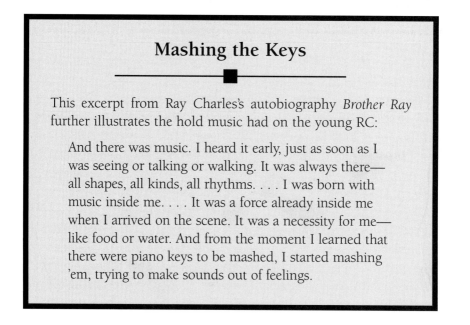

Mashing the Keys

This excerpt from Ray Charles's autobiography *Brother Ray* further illustrates the hold music had on the young RC:

> And there was music. I heard it early, just as soon as I was seeing or talking or walking. It was always there— all shapes, all kinds, all rhythms. . . . I was born with music inside me. . . . It was a force already inside me when I arrived on the scene. It was a necessity for me— like food or water. And from the moment I learned that there were piano keys to be mashed, I started mashing 'em, trying to make sounds out of feelings.

wallow in dependency. Determined to teach him to take care of himself, she insisted that RC do everything he had done before—even chores like chopping wood.

RC later recalled that many of their neighbors were horrified by Aretha's actions; they were convinced that she was torturing a helpless blind boy. Nonetheless, as he later recalled, his mother trusted her instincts and persevered: "You know, my mother, she was not an educated woman, [but] she had . . . I don't know what kind of sense you would call it. We used to call it horse sense, common sense, mother wit, you know. She had, I think, as much of that as God could possibly stick in anybody's brain."[11]

Because RC's blindness was gradual, he and Aretha had time to develop ways to compensate for his lack of vision. As he remembered it, his mother would tell him, "You might not be able to do things like a person who can see. But there are always two ways to do everything. You've just got to find the other way."[12] He further recalled,

> My mother . . . had a strong feeling about independence. Just because I was blind, she'd tell me, didn't mean I was stupid. "One of these days I'm gonna die and you're gonna have to take care of yourself," she'd say. So I was taught to wash and scrub and cook and rake the yard and make my own bed. . . . If I hadn't of been taught by my mother, I wouldn't be anywhere.[13]

Florida D&B

Aretha had already taught RC the alphabet and basic arithmetic skills. She now set her sights on formal education for the boy in addition to the practical life skills she taught him. But Retha had only a rudimentary education herself, and it became clear that her abilities as an academic teacher were limited. Furthermore, the schools in Greenville were not equipped to teach a blind child. Aretha tackled this problem with characteristic energy and determination. With the help of a sympathetic white family, she learned of a state-run facility, the Florida School for the Deaf and Blind. Florida D&B, as it was known, was located in the town of St. Augustine, on the state's northeast coast.

Each year, the school accepted a few "colored" students (as African Americans were then called). In fact, Aretha learned, there was an opening for the term beginning in the fall of 1937. Furthermore, it would cost her nothing—the state would take care of all expenses, even the train fare to St. Augustine.

Aretha was enthusiastic about the opportunity, but Mary Jane was reluctant to make the boy leave familiar surroundings. For

A conductor on a Florida train signals from the rear car reserved for African Americans. At the age of seven, Charles traveled on such a segregated train when he left home to attend school in St. Augustine.

his part, young RC—only seven—was terrified of going alone to an unknown city, leaving his family and the only home he knew. However, his strong-willed mother prevailed, and in October 1937, having just turned seven, RC boarded a train. The conductor looked after the boy on the train, and a teacher met him at the St. Augustine station for the trip to his new home.

Starting School

Florida D&B was in many ways a grim place, especially for its black students. Their strictly segregated facilities were cramped and poor compared to those for whites. One shabby building housed everything—classrooms, dormitories, dining room, laundry, and so on—for the school's ninety African American students, of whom about sixty were boys.

Equipment and supplies for the black students, such as typewriters, sewing machines, and books, were similarly poor in quality. Most were hand-me-downs from the school's 300-odd white students. The curriculum for the black students was equally low-grade; though there were classes in music and other topics, most of the curriculum was geared toward learning broommaking and other simple manual skills.

RC's life at the school did not begin happily. For one thing, he was teased mercilessly by older boys. They mocked him because he was so poor that he had to wear clothes donated by the state, and they called him "Foots" because he had no shoes. They also made fun of him because he was lonely and cried often. However, at least one good thing came out of RC's first months at Florida D&B: He quickly mastered Braille, the system of raised dots that enables blind people to read by touch.

The First Year

RC's loneliness grew worse at Christmas. Aretha could not afford to bring her son home for the holiday break, and the state did not pay for travel except at the end of the year. RC thus had to spend the entire two weeks of vacation on campus with no other students around. He was even more intensely lonely than he had been at the start of the school year. "And, baby," he wrote in his autobiography, "when everyone had gone home for the holidays and I was left alone, I was *really* alone. That was something I wasn't ever gonna forget. . . . I cried my little eyes out those weeks."[14]

Early in the new year, RC experienced more problems. His right eye began to throb unbearably with pain, and the school's doctor ordered it removed. The boy spent much of the spring recuperating from the operation.

When he was able to attend classes again, RC fell into a regular routine with the other students. The boys, who all slept in the same room, got up at 5:30 and washed. Then they lined up in the hall, the deaf in one line and the blind in another, to file in for breakfast. Boys were chosen in rotation to say a blessing over the food, which typically consisted of grits or oatmeal and milk; orange juice was a special treat once a week.

Then came chapel, a round of classes, "one o'clock dinner," and more classes. Supper, the evening meal, typically consisted of starchy food like spaghetti or bread with corn syrup. The students' precious free time in the evenings was spent playing games or listening to the dorm's single radio, usually tuned to baseball games or music broadcasts.

End of the School Year

Once he became accustomed to life at school, RC proved a good student. He excelled at math, he loved machinery and could take apart and repair radios, and he learned to type seventy-five words a minute (on a regular typewriter) with no mistakes. The boy constantly got into mischief, however, and sometimes risked serious trouble. One such incident stemmed from RC's love of machinery, which led him to drive a teacher's car around the campus at night while a deaf kid sat on the hood, banging his fists to give directions left or right. RC did well until he backed up and hit a tree; the collision knocked him out of the car's open cab. He lay on the ground, stunned, until a friend shook him into action and they could get away.

Another incident of troublemaking came when RC was unable to play a music exercise correctly and a teacher rapped the boy's knuckles with a ruler, typical classroom discipline at the time. Instinctively, RC lashed out and hit her. The school principal, furious, was prepared to expel him. Fortunately, the teacher intervened and requested leniency; RC received a lesser, more suitable punishment.

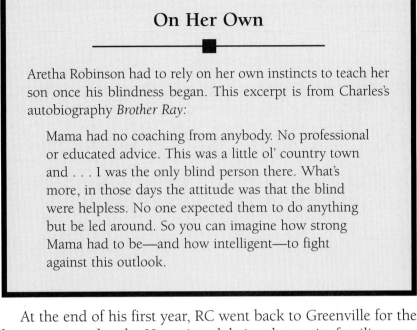

On Her Own

Aretha Robinson had to rely on her own instincts to teach her son once his blindness began. This excerpt is from Charles's autobiography *Brother Ray:*

> Mama had no coaching from anybody. No professional or educated advice. This was a little ol' country town and . . . I was the only blind person there. What's more, in those days the attitude was that the blind were helpless. No one expected them to do anything but be led around. So you can imagine how strong Mama had to be—and how intelligent—to fight against this outlook.

At the end of his first year, RC went back to Greenville for the long summer break. He enjoyed being home in familiar surroundings, where he was treated with special attention by Aretha, Mary Jane, and his neighbors. He played happily with his old friends, spending his days in pastimes such as riding bicycles. (He steered by listening to the sound of his tires or feeling the grass at the side of the road as it hit his legs.)

Of course, he also played the piano and listened to the jukebox at Mr. Pit's. This continuing love of music was about to assume a dominant role in RC's life. During his coming year at Florida D&B, he started to concentrate on his musical destiny.

Chapter Two

The School of the Road

Listen here, I say to myself, 'tain't much you can do about this here situation. So you better just continue to continue.

—RAY CHARLES ON BEING BLIND AND ON HIS OWN

During his first year at Florida D&B, RC had taken only a casual interest in the music lessons offered there. For one thing, competition for time on the school's single practice piano was fierce, and older kids had priority. Charles recalled in his autobiography that, for him, music at D&B during that first year had simply been a lark: "I'd wander over to the rooms where the big boys or the big girls were practicing the piano. I'd love to just hang around and listen. I was always on the prowl for new sounds. I tried to copy anything I heard just for the fun of it."[15]

During his second year, however, RC became more serious about music and began taking formal classes. The school's music teacher, Mrs. Lawrence, did not like the rough boogie-woogie that RC had learned in Greenville. "The gut-bucket music might have been our own," he later remarked, "but it was not tolerated during lessons."[16]

Instead, Mrs. Lawrence taught him the elements of classical technique. RC liked the classical music he learned (except for Bach—the busy, contrasting lines made him nervous). He also realized quickly that classical technique would be an excellent foundation for a well-rounded musical education, since it would teach him proper fingering and theory. However, he also recognized the limitations of written classical music and its differences from improvised jazz:

> Classical music is fixed, a cinch. You put [Beethoven's] *Moonlight Sonata* in front of you and you get to play it the way he wrote it. [But] jazz is for expressing yourself. It's not packaged on a silver platter. You improvise. All you have is a foundation, a jumping-off point, and as far as you can fly depends on how strong your wings are.[17]

Focusing

Among other things, Mrs. Lawrence taught RC how to read and write Braille music notation. This system was effective but cumbersome; a piano student could learn only a few bars of a piece at a time, since he needed one hand to read while playing with the other before switching to learn the other hand's part. It took a long time to combine the two parts into a single entity. However, RC found a positive side to Braille music notation: It forced him to strengthen his powers of recall and analysis. He commented, "You can't play it and see it at the same time, so your memory and understanding expand."[18]

In addition to his formal studies, RC spent as much time as possible listening to the radio with other like-minded kids. Exposed in this way to dozens of artists, he formed a lasting love for the work of a number of musicians. One was Art Tatum, a brilliant, partially blind, fleet-fingered pianist who would remain RC's lifelong idol.

RC also regularly heard broadcasts by big bands. In addition to the acknowledged giants of this genre, like Ellington, Basie, and Benny Goodman, RC was especially drawn to a white musician, clarinetist Artie Shaw. He was so intrigued by the expressive sound of Shaw's "licorice stick" that he took up the clarinet in addition to his main instrument.

RC sometimes sang as well. Singing came naturally to him, since he had always sung in church on Sundays. But the piano remained RC's first love, and in time he became the school's dominant piano player. Kids clamored to hear him play and sing popular tunes of the day. He regularly accompanied other students at the music department's weekly recitals. And two or three times a year, he and a drummer played for the school's social dances.

Tallahassee

Most of RC's summer vacations were spent in Greenville, but he began spending part of each long break in Tallahassee, the state

Jazz musician Art Tatum performs in New York City in 1944. Partially blind, the brilliant musician served as an inspiration to the young Ray Charles.

Artie Shaw plays a solo on his clarinet during a 1939 performance. Ray Charles was particularly drawn to Shaw's music.

capital. He roomed with the Johnsons, family friends who had relocated from Greenville. The bigger city excited the young man for several reasons; one was that he learned to ride a motorbike there. "I had always been nervy," he later remarked about such daring stunts, "and I always had a lot of faith in my ability not to break my neck." [19]

Mainly, however, Tallahassee was exciting because it gave RC, now a teenager, his first taste of professional musicianship. The opportunity came through Lawyer Smith, a baker who also led the city's foremost working jazz band. Smith liked the confident blind kid and hired him whenever possible. RC generally stayed in the background, playing just rhythm accompaniment, but sometimes he was given a feature—the chance to play and sing a number as a solo act, backed up by the band.

Smith's group played a regular circuit of clubs and bars around town, as well as gatherings such as parties, dances, and weddings. The environment provided a big-city thrill that the pianist, barely into his teens, had never felt before. Biographer Michael Lydon notes that RC relished the experience immensely: "He took right away to the smoke and the loose laughter, hanging out with the cats, the music hot and cool."[20]

Aretha's Death

Back at school, as one of the older students, RC was allowed greater freedom. He began exploring St. Augustine. He walked everywhere, never using a cane or a guide dog. He found his way by recognizing the distinctive sounds of streets and noting any obstacles he encountered, such as drainage pipes or cracks in the sidewalk.

And, because he was an older student, RC was also allowed to play occasionally at semiprofessional gigs. These typically were afternoon tea parties and ladies' club socials held by well-to-do residents of the city. On one occasion, the budding musician even broadcast live on WFOY, the local radio station.

Then, in 1945, personal tragedy struck: Aretha Robinson died at the age of 31. Food poisoning was apparently the immediate cause; however, she had never been physically robust and the poisoning may have aggravated an existing illness. Her son later remarked that there was little anyone could have done: "There were just no medical facilities outside of the local doctor. The nearest hospital was forty miles (64km) away, in Georgia."[21]

Leaving School

Thunderstruck by his mother's sudden death, RC was deeply depressed for a long time: "I couldn't cry right then, and I couldn't eat for three weeks, and I almost died for it."[22] The boy spent the rest of the summer alone in Greenville, inconsolable: "'I'm not always gonna be with you.' Those were Mama's words, and I can't tell you how many times she must have said

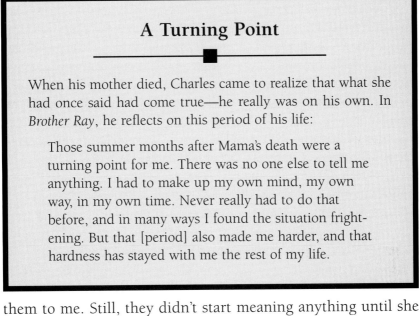

A Turning Point

When his mother died, Charles came to realize that what she had once said had come true—he really was on his own. In *Brother Ray*, he reflects on this period of his life:

Those summer months after Mama's death were a turning point for me. There was no one else to tell me anything. I had to make up my own mind, my own way, in my own time. Never really had to do that before, and in many ways I found the situation frightening. But that [period] also made me harder, and that hardness has stayed with me the rest of my life.

them to me. Still, they didn't start meaning anything until she was gone."[23]

During his hours of solitude, RC decided that he was outgrowing school, that Florida D&B had nothing more to teach him. He knew he had to make his own way; Mary Jane loved him, but there was little she could do for him financially. Moreover, RC sensed that, whatever his future might be, it would not involve the manual skills Florida D&B stressed. As he put it, "I didn't want to spend my life makin' brooms."[24]

The situation resolved itself quickly. Two weeks into the new term, RC got into trouble by provoking a teacher. He was either expelled or quit; accounts vary. In either case, the last entry on his official student card read, "Sent home Oct. 5, 1945. Unsatisfactory pupil."[25]

Jacksonville

Barely fifteen, RC was now on his own. But he did not go back to Greenville or live with other relatives; the desire for self-sufficiency was too strong. He remarked later, "My mother had brainwashed me to the point where I had to be independent. There was no point in living off this aunt or that uncle, and anyway they was mostly living in places like Baltimore, which was a long way away."[26]

Instead, he accepted an offer from his mother's friends Lena Mae and Fred Thompson. The Thompsons lived in Jacksonville, fifty miles (80km) north of St. Augustine and, at the time, the biggest city in Florida. They had an extra room for rent, and RC moved in to try his luck as a working musician.

The Thompsons had no children and welcomed the young man into their house. They wanted to help him financially, but RC was determined to pay his own way. To this end, Fred Thompson helped him join the "colored musicians'" union, Local 632. RC quickly memorized the route to the union offices and walked there every afternoon looking for a pickup gig—that is, a job as a casual, last-minute addition to a band.

Jamming

The young musician also sat in on jam sessions whenever possible. Jam sessions are informal gatherings typically frequented by jazz musicians with nonmusical day jobs or jobs in musically unchallenging bands. Frequently held late at night, these sessions give musicians a chance to stretch out, play the music they like, and exercise rarely used musical "muscles."

But then as now, jam sessions were tricky. The songs played were usually standards, with familiar melodies and chord progressions. However, musicians relished making things wickedly difficult, playing even a simple tune at a breakneck tempo or in an unusual key. Top players tried to best each other in "cutting contests" of skill, inventiveness, and verve.

For RC, jam sessions were good for making contacts in the local music scene. They were even more useful for honing his chops—that is, improving his skills. Jams taught RC vital techniques such as reacting quickly to changes in tempo, transposing fluently into different keys, and expressing himself in solos.

It helped that he had perfect pitch; that is, he could hear a note and know if it was a high C or a G flat. Also, RC's hearing was so sharp that he could easily distinguish each instrument. (A longtime associate once remarked, "He'd know it if the bass

Ray Charles tickles the keys during a recorded jam session. Such sessions allowed Charles to hone his musical skills and to establish contacts in the local music scene.

missed a note, a single note. He'd know it if the drummer's left shoelace was flapping."[27]) Furthermore, he could visualize chord and song structures in his head, so that even the most complex music came easily.

These skills helped RC hold his own in the most intense cutting contests. "Real musicians weren't pampered," Charles recalled of his days in Jacksonville. "They figured out what they had to do, and then they went out and did it. Sure, it was cruel and hard-nosed, but, baby, you did learn to play."[28]

Getting Gigs

As word of his growing skill got around, RC began getting pickup work for two or three dollars a night. A fellow musician,

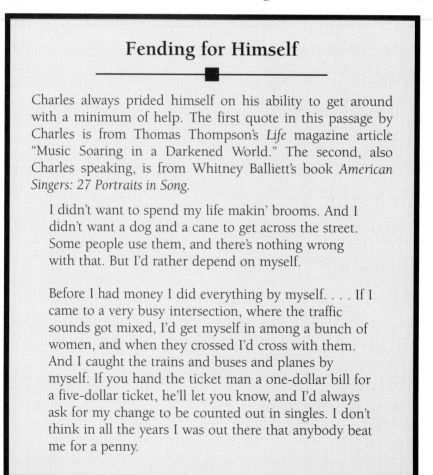

Fending for Himself

Charles always prided himself on his ability to get around with a minimum of help. The first quote in this passage by Charles is from Thomas Thompson's *Life* magazine article "Music Soaring in a Darkened World." The second, also Charles speaking, is from Whitney Balliett's book *American Singers: 27 Portraits in Song*.

> I didn't want to spend my life makin' brooms. And I didn't want a dog and a cane to get across the street. Some people use them, and there's nothing wrong with that. But I'd rather depend on myself.

> Before I had money I did everything by myself. . . . If I came to a very busy intersection, where the traffic sounds got mixed, I'd get myself in among a bunch of women, and when they crossed I'd cross with them. And I caught the trains and buses and planes by myself. If you hand the ticket man a one-dollar bill for a five-dollar ticket, he'll let you know, and I'd always ask for my change to be counted out in singles. I don't think in all the years I was out there that anybody beat me for a penny.

Alexander Perry, was a member of the same union during this period. He recalled the wide variety of jobs they typically played: "We played everywhere in those days. One night a white place where we'd go in through the kitchen and play behind a curtain [hidden from the well-to-do white patrons], the next night a whorehouse where they played cards and drank moonshine."[29]

Soon, RC had two semiregular jobs. One was as a substitute pianist in a group led by Alvin Downing that played six nights a week at Manuel's Tap Room; the band's pay was steady but low, and when Downing's pianist took a better-paying gig, which was often, the bandleader hired RC. The teen's other engagement, with Henry Washington's band at the elegant Two Spot Club, paid better but occurred less frequently.

Even with the sporadic pay, RC loved life in the heady world of Jacksonville jazz. He was a kid, but he was moving fast in a world of adults. He recalled, "Everyone . . . seemed at least five to ten years older than me. And I was impressed with the idea of being able to play in a nightclub till midnight, or maybe even later. That was a big deal to a kid."[30]

New Styles

As RC settled into the Jacksonville scene, however, popular music was undergoing change. Both Downing's and Washington's groups were big bands, but this style was beginning to fall out of favor. After more than a decade of intense popularity, big bands were being replaced by smaller combos.

Some of these small groups played a modified version of the big band sound. Others favored an intense, intellectual new kind of jazz called bebop. Still others played a funkier style, half blues and half jazz, that stressed wailing saxophones, bluesy vocals, and highly danceable rhythms. *Billboard*, a prominent industry magazine, gave this music a name: rhythm and blues, or R&B. And still another style of music coming into favor was a smooth, sophisticated jazz-pop exemplified by two pianist-singers, Nat "King" Cole and Charles Brown.

RC was not interested in bebop, but he loved R&B and idolized both Cole and Brown. The teen realized that the ability to play well in such crowd-pleasing styles meant steadier and more prominent work, so he worked on his R&B chops and tried hard to emulate Cole and Brown. He was rewarded with occasional feature spots for songs like Brown's big hit, "Driftin' Blues."

Down and Out in Orlando

RC was by now eager to explore new territory beyond Jacksonville, and R&B was his ticket out. The pianist joined the band of Tiny York, a locally popular singer and saxophonist, for a tour of the clubs of central Florida. It was not a successful trip, however; the gigs dried up after a few weeks and the band was stranded in Orlando.

RC could have ridden back to Jacksonville with the rest of the band—after they had raised enough gas money—but instead he made a bold decision: He stayed in Orlando. At sixteen, he was now totally on his own, with no nearby friends or familiar surroundings.

At the time, Orlando was a small town with only a handful of clubs that held out the prospect of work for a piano player. Jobs were not forthcoming, and the young musician nearly starved. It was a major tragedy when one day he dropped a jar of preserves and it smashed on the floor. Charles recalled later the "times when I was sustaining myself on beans and water and crackers, and it came to be a heavy proposition—a malnutrition thing."[31]

Better Luck

Slowly, though, RC established himself and began getting gigs at outdoor fish fries and small roadhouses. These modest affairs paid only a few dollars or a meal. They could be dangerous, too, RC recalled: "I tried to find the location of a window as soon as I started working a new place. If a fire or a hot brawl started up, I wanted to know how to escape."[32]

In the spring of 1947, RC finally got a regular job with the house band at Orlando's top nightspot, the Sunshine Club. He proved so capable that he was soon arranging for the band—that is, writing out music charts that specified what each musician played. Some groups relied on stock arrangements bought as sheet music, but original charts were better because they sounded fresher.

Most musicians used pencil and blank sheet music to write arrangements, but RC could not. Nor was Braille musical nota-

Nat "King" Cole embodied a distinctive jazz-pop style that Ray Charles worked hard to emulate.

Ray Charles reads music from a Braille score. Instead of relying on Braille music, however, Charles usually arranged music in his head, which he then dictated to a sighted person.

tion useful in this case: Putting down an arrangement in Braille was time-consuming and complicated and the notation could not be understood by sighted musicians who could only read print music. So RC worked out in his mind each instrument's part, then dictated this arrangement to another musician who copied it down conventionally.

Arranging was just one of several important musical steps forward that RC took in Orlando. He also composed his first song, "Confession Blues." And he began playing alto sax, having switched from the clarinet (a somewhat similar instrument) because the sax's bolder sound was more easily heard over a wailing R&B band.

Tampa

Things were looking up, but there were also disappointments. First came the news that RC's father, Bailey, had died; now the pianist was truly an orphan. Then RC was crushed when he failed to impress a prominent national bandleader, Lucky Millinder, who was passing through town.

By the summer of 1947, disappointed at his overall luck, the restless RC pulled up stakes again. A friend had offered him a ride to Tampa, on Florida's Gulf coast. Almost immediately, RC ran into an acquaintance, guitarist Garcia "Gossie" McKee, whom he had known in Jacksonville. (Some sources list the musician's first name as Gosady.)

Gossie found RC a room to rent and introduced him around, and by the fall the pianist had steady gigs with two Tampa bands. One was Charlie Brantley's Honeydrippers, a popular R&B band. The other was more unusual: a white country group called the Florida Playboys.

The latter job came about after RC became friendly with a Tampa record store clerk who also was a Playboy. RC fit in right away; there were apparently no major incidents because of his race. Also, playing country was technically easy compared to jazz; and, perhaps, most important, he knew and genuinely liked the music. RC once remarked about his love for country music, "It was honest music, not cleaned up, and it still is. They don't sing, 'I sat there and dreamed of you'; they say, 'I missed you and I went out and got drunk.'"[33]

Northward Bound

The Playboys paid $15 or $20 a night, and Brantley's band about $10 a night—decent money for the time and place. Things got even better after RC began a steady gig with the Manzy Harris Quartet, which played for white audiences at Tampa's high-class Skyhaven Club. This job paid a whopping $30 nightly.

RC was able to send much of his earnings to a bank in Greenville, and with the extra cash he started making long-range plans. He and Gossie had been talking about trying their luck somewhere far from Florida. Big cities like New York, Chicago, and Los Angeles were daunting, so they looked at a map and started considering other towns.

In Constant Motion

In this passage from his book *American Singers: 27 Portraits in Song*, jazz writer Whitney Balliett describes Charles's restless energy and physical impression:

His appearance is deceptive. From a distance, he looks frail and spidery. He has a shuffling, bent-kneed walk, and at the piano he sways wildly from side to side or rears back to the point of falling over. A steady smile and big, ever-present dark glasses mask his face and make him seem smaller than he is. But close up he is tough and compact. He has wide, boxer's shoulders and a flat, trim waist, a high forehead, close-cropped hair, flaring cheekbones, and a jutting, stony chin. His speaking voice is deep and gutteral and hand-hewn. He talks quickly and his language moves between sunny, sprawling Southern colloquialisms and lofty Northern abstractions. He is startling on the telephone; he literally barks and grunts. And he is in constant motion—reading from a Braille notebook with one hand and holding a telephone with the other, lifting his head and shooting out his chin, wringing his hands or clapping them softly together, and standing up for no reason to do a little hopping dance and then abruptly sitting down.

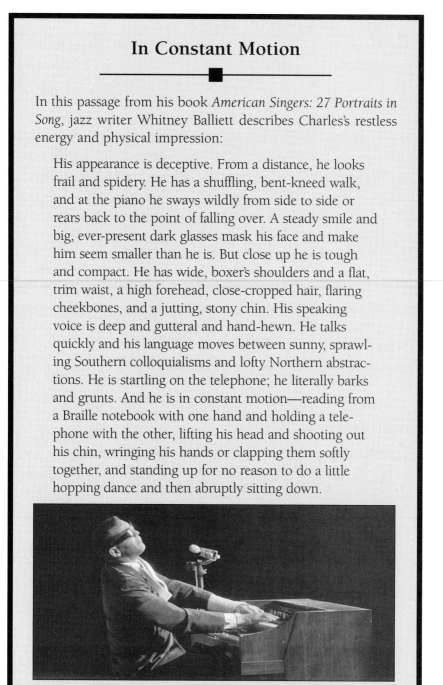

During a 1961 performance, Ray Charles exhibits the unbounded on-stage energy for which he was famous.

According to legend, RC chose Seattle, Washington, because that was the farthest he could go in the continental United States from Florida. He recalled,

> I didn't know anyone living up there, and I hadn't heard a thing about the town. It just seemed like a reasonable place to go. All mystery and adventure. I also liked the fact that it was way on the other coast—real far away. That term—West Coast—was appealing to me. I came from the woods, and the idea of heading west was enticing as hell.[34]

According to some sources, however, the story is slightly different. In this version, the reason for choosing Seattle was romantic. Gossie had recently met a Canadian woman who was moving to Vancouver, British Columbia. He suggested Seattle—the nearest American city of any size to Vancouver—in order to be close to her.

RC, however, had his own romance to think about. He had been dating a woman named Louise and was reluctant to leave Florida. Gossie finally convinced him by pointing out that in a northern city like Seattle he could date white women, an impossibility in color-conscious Florida. (Louise was apparently not the only female RC found attractive.)

The pianist agreed to head for Seattle, but he wanted to spend a little more time with Louise. Gossie went first and RC left about a week later, taking with him some $500 in savings. Always thrifty, he survived on crackers and candy bars during the long, dull bus ride. This journey marked the start of a new era: RC Robinson was about to become Ray Charles.

Chapter Three

From Obscurity to Stardom

Gospel and the blues are really, if you break it down, almost the same thing. It's just a question of whether you're talkin' about a woman or God.

—RAY CHARLES

ON THE SIMILARITIES OF THE MUSICAL STYLES HE MERGED

RC arrived in Seattle in March 1948 and found Gossie living in a hotel in the heart of the Central District, Seattle's black neighborhood. "The CD" was lively in those booming postwar years, bolstered by Seattle's flourishing port and aerospace industry; its clubs and restaurants promised plenty of work for the ambitious musicians.

They performed as a duo and, with bassist Milton Garred, in a trio. Calling themselves the McSon Trio (the name combined McKee and Robinson), they soon had steady work at places like the Rocking Chair Club and the Elks Club, and even appeared on one of the Seattle area's first live television broadcasts. In addition, the trio bought fifteen minutes of radio time every week, playing and giving out McKee's phone number to boost their publicity.

The trio quickly developed a strong reputation—especially its keyboard man. It was clear to all that RC's abilities far outpaced those of the locals. Typical was a comment by bassist Traff Hubert: "We knew right away this RC Robinson was the best pianist in the Northwest."[35] Melody Jones, another key figure on the Seattle scene, added, "We were astounded at how young he was and how well he played."[36]

When RC sang during a gig, it was his version of Nat Cole's and Charles Brown's jazz-pop. For a laugh, though, he sometimes performed in a rowdy style strongly reminiscent of gospel. Seattle bassist Buddy Catlett recalls, "It wasn't until after he went to Los Angeles that he began that gospel style [seriously]. Here, he would only do that for fun. I mean, gospel was [for] church. It was sacrilegious [to sing it elsewhere]. So he would like poke fun at it. I didn't know he was serious!"[37]

In the late 1940s, Quincy Jones, a young trumpeter, met Ray Charles in Seattle, and the two became fast friends.

Coming of Age

RC's time in Seattle—which he likened to the Jewish ceremony called a bar mitzvah, when a boy ritually becomes a man—encompassed several significant events. One concerned his name. He had always been Ray or RC Robinson, but he wanted to avoid confusion with a famous boxer, Sugar Ray Robinson. Professionally, therefore, Ray Charles Robinson became simply Ray Charles.

Also, as his prominence on the Seattle jazz scene increased, the pianist lived better than ever before. Louise joined him, and they had a nice house with a telephone, a piano, and a hi-fi record player. RC's place became a hangout for musicians, including a teenage trumpeter named Quincy Jones. The two formed a close friendship that continued long after Jones achieved his own fame.

Charlie Parker jams on the saxophone during a 1949 concert. Parker and singer Billie Holiday glamorized heroin use among jazz musicians in the 1940s.

A third significant event during RC's Seattle sojourn was his introduction to heroin. The drug was popular among jazz musicians, in part because such giants as Charlie Parker and Billie Holiday had glamorized its use; the justification was that it dramatically improved one's playing. Always curious, RC experimented and was soon using heroin regularly, getting others to help him prepare and inject it.

The First Records

In Seattle, Charles also broke into recording. Late in 1948 Jack Lauderdale, the owner of a small Los Angeles record company, heard the McSon Trio. Lauderdale was impressed, especially with the pianist, and signed the group. Its first recording was Charles's "Confession Blues" and, on the record's flip (other) side, "I Love You, I Love You," written by a friend of the pianist.

The record, cut in Seattle, was released early in 1949 on Down Beat Records. Although the record's label mistakenly identified the group as the "Maxin Trio," the group was thrilled. Other Seattle musicians were impressed as well; trumpeter Floyd Standifer commented, "A record on an L.A. label was a big deal. We kept asking ourselves, that cat's been here [only] a year, how can he have a record?"[38]

"Confession Blues" sold well in Seattle and even made a tiny dent in the national sales charts. Lauderdale wanted more tunes and flew McKee and Charles to Los Angeles for the sessions; it was the first time either had been in a plane. The invitation did not extend to Garred, whose performance and attitude were unpredictable; a studio musician replaced him.

Leaving Seattle

Back in Seattle, Charles grew restless. The pianist—clearly the most talented member of the McSon Trio—was leaning toward becoming a solo act. Tensions within the group grew and the trio began to drift apart. RC's personal life also was unsettled; Louise missed Tampa and her family, and she and Charles fought often. In the spring of 1950, she went back to Florida.

Soon after this, Charles returned to Los Angeles to make his first records as Ray Charles. On his earlier trip, the singer had not had time to explore the city, but this time he did—and found its vibrant music scene, large black community, and warm weather to his liking. He decided to stay.

It was a good move. Before long, Charles was a rising star, making decent money in the clubs and with a hit record, "Baby, Let Me Hold Your Hand," climbing the charts. His romantic life also improved: Charles dated a number of women, thus beginning a lifelong habit of conducting multiple, simultaneous love affairs.

Joining Fulson

Although Charles was successful as a solo act, Lauderdale suggested that he also join the band of a more prominent musician. This was blues guitarist and singer Lowell Fulson, who, like Charles, recorded on the Down Beat label. The match was a good one, and the partnership was sealed when Charles played on a Fulson record, "Every Day I Have the Blues," that became a million-selling hit.

Charles remained in Fulson's band for a series of tours through the South and Southwest. In addition to playing piano, RC was the band's musical director, writing charts and otherwise maintaining musical order in the group. Charles also had a solo spot in each show when he sang his current solo hits.

During this period, Charles signed on with a manager, New York–based Shaw Agency. This was a significant move. Now he had a New York agent, a Los Angeles record label, and a featured spot in a top blues band. He was ripe for national exposure.

On the Road

But working on the road, even with a popular band, was grueling. Besides enduring endless hours on an old bus, touring the strictly segregated South meant dealing with nonstop indignities and discomfort off the bus as well.

For example, the few hotels and restaurants open to African Americans were usually shoddy. Periodic encounters with violent racists also created a constant threat of danger. Stanley Turrentine, a saxophonist in Fulson's band, recalled, "We put our lives in jeopardy going out to play our music. We clung together tight, because our lives depended on each guy watching out for the other."[39]

Ray Charles (left) performs with the McSon Trio while on tour in the 1950s. Touring the segregated South was a grueling experience for Charles.

Despite such problems, however, Charles adapted easily to life on the road. For one thing, he rarely lacked for romantic company. The singer had girlfriends in many cities, and in 1951 he married one: Eileen Williams, a beautician from Ohio. She traveled with him, but the marriage did not last and they soon parted.

Charles needed only minimal help on the road. For example, he had friends organize his wallet so that he always knew what bills he used. He maintained a phone book, using a deck of cards marked in Braille as its "pages." He even played cards, using a special deck marked in Braille. (However, he was not allowed to deal the cards out, since he could have identified them by touch!)

First Impressions

Jerry Wexler of Atlantic Records would be a major catalyst for Charles's breakthrough R&B records of the 1950s. In this excerpt from his memoir *Rhythm and the Blues: A Life in American Music*, Wexler describes their first meeting:

Our first encounter was in our office over Patsy's Restaurant. I was struck by his physical presence: strong, broad-shouldered, and barrel-chested, his rhythms simultaneously quick and cautious. Though led by an assistant, once inside a room Ray took no time to suss [figure] out the configurations, thereafter moving as one who'd seen all along. His speaking voice, like his singing voice, was deep but everchanging, sometimes sounding old beyond his years, sometimes filled with youthful ebullience, sometimes sullen and withdrawn.

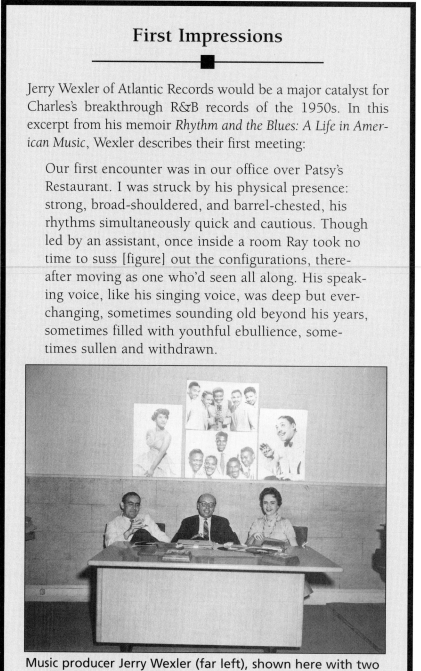

Music producer Jerry Wexler (far left), shown here with two Atlantic Records colleagues, was a major contributor to Charles's success in the 1950s.

Traveling for any length of time on the tour bus was demanding, however, and Charles grew tired of the enforced closeness. Always careful with money, he saved enough to buy a car and hire a driver. After that, he no longer had to ride in the distraction-filled bus. In the privacy of his car, he could spend the long hours locked in his private thoughts, writing songs, scoring charts, or listening to the radio.

Atlantic

Charles continued to nurse solo ambitions and made several more records under his own name. The pianist, who was much more sophisticated musically than the bandleader, began demanding increasingly steep raises. This did not endear him to Fulson; their relations soured, and Charles made serious plans to go solo.

Meanwhile, Charles's label, Swingtime (the name had changed from Down Beat), was in financial trouble. Lauderdale, its owner, needed to concentrate on his most popular artists, not a relative unknown like Charles. He put Charles's contract up for sale, and it was bought for $2,500 by Atlantic, a small, scrappy New York City label with a growing track record for R&B hits.

Charles quit the Fulson band in 1952 and in the fall of that year made his first recordings for Atlantic. These were done in Atlantic's makeshift studio, which served as the company's offices during the day. The space was so tight that desks had to be pushed aside to make room for instruments.

"Should Win Some Attention"

With a small band behind him, Charles recorded four tunes during that session. They were varied stylistically. Three imitated established sounds—those of Nat Cole, Charles Brown, and Jimmy Rushing, who sang with Count Basie's band.

But the fourth, "The Sun's Gonna Shine Again," was a conscious effort to forge an original style. Charles had always been flattered when people told him he sounded like Brown or Cole, but he was also beginning to wonder what it would be like "if people began to recognize *me*, if they'd tell me I sounded like Ray Charles."[40]

Atlantic's executives, Ahmet Ertegun and Herb Abramson, liked the distinctive song best. However, they made what they felt was a safer choice for Charles's first Atlantic release: the Cole-influenced "Roll with My Baby," backed with the Brown sounda-like "Midnight Hour." *Billboard* magazine reviewed the record favorably with its characteristic slangy prose: "Charles goes to town on this rollicking rhythm opus for a spirited effort. Platter should do right fine in the coin boxes . . . . Should win some attention."[41]

Two Hits

Despite this breezy prediction, however, the record did poorly. By contrast, Charles's next release, the more original "The Sun's Gonna Shine Again," sold fairly well. Encouraged, Ertegun and Abramson began urging the singer to continue developing his style. This enthusiasm for fresh sounds grew even stronger when a new producer joined Atlantic—Jerry Wexler, a former *Billboard* journalist who had coined the very term "rhythm and blues."

Charles's follow-up efforts to "The Sun's Gonna Shine Again" sold decently but not brilliantly. Meanwhile, the singer maintained a busy tour schedule, mostly in the South. In New Orleans, he connected with blues guitarist and singer Eddie Lee Jones, better known as Guitar Slim. With Charles, Slim recorded a smash hit record, "The Things I Used to Do," which reached the coveted #1 spot on the *Billboard* charts in 1954.

This was the second time Charles had performed on someone else's smash. But that same year Charles scored his own national hit for the first time: the breezy romp "It Shoulda Been Me." *Billboard* characterized this clever song as "Charles' hottest disking to date."[42]

His Own Voice

By now, Charles's habit of imitating others was nearly gone. Although still influenced by jazz, the blues, R&B, and gospel, the singer was blending them in original ways. His singing voice was also becoming more soulful and honest, playful and strong. Jerry Wexler, the Atlantic producer, described it as "a startling cry— direct, raw, riveted with feeling."[43]

Part of the power of Charles's recordings stemmed from this powerful voice. Another important factor was Charles's habit of

Singing Around the News

———————■———————

Producers Jerry Wexler and Ahmet Ertegun flew to Atlanta, Georgia, in 1954 to record what would become Charles's break-through early singles. In a memorial article called "Remembering Ray" in *Rolling Stone*, Wexler recalls the occasion:

> We did the session at WGST, the campus radio station at Georgia Tech. He did "I've Got a Woman," "Come Back Baby," "Greenbacks" and one other song. There was this elderly engineer who didn't know a damn thing about what he was supposed to do. It was three hours before we could get the sound right in the studio. Then we had to stop every hour so they could broadcast the news—the control room was the newsroom. But out of this, we got those songs, the definitive beginnings of *the* Ray Charles.

overseeing virtually every aspect of the process. He wrote most of his own material and always arranged it; unlike many singers, he was never pressured by his company to record certain songs in certain ways. Furthermore, curious as ever about things mechanical and electrical, Charles learned recording engineering, which gave him the ability to fine-tune his sound from the recording booth.

The result was that the singer soon became his own producer. Officially, Jerry Wexler and Ahmet Ertegun filled this role, but they freely admitted they did little. Wexler commented, "I realized that the best thing I could do with Ray was leave him alone."[44] Ertegun added, "Ray . . . was becoming a great recording artist before our eyes, an artist fully aware of his medium."[45]

Della

During this period, Charles's personal life took a major turn. In 1954, during an interview at a radio station in Houston, the singer mentioned that he loved a local gospel group, the Cecil

Shaw Singers. A member of the group, Della Beatrice Howard, heard the broadcast and called the station. Would Charles like to meet Cecil Shaw? Yes, he replied—and could he meet the young lady too?

When they met, Charles was powerfully attracted. B, as Charles called her, was sweet and quiet, a high school graduate

The backbone of Ray Charles's first permanent band came from a group he assembled to back singer Ruth Brown on a tour of Texas in 1954

and devout Christian who did not smoke or drink. Charles courted her, but he was reluctant to settle in Houston; he disliked its humid climate and history of racism, and he was eager to separate Della from her protective family. He convinced her to move to Dallas, where they were married in 1955.

Meanwhile, Charles was realizing a long-held dream: the formation of his own permanent band. For years, he had struggled with pickup bands, using casual players hired in whatever city he played. But these were often terrible musicians; the final straw, he recalled, came in Philadelphia: "Man, I love music and I hate to hear it played wrong . . . . I [played] a club in Philly and the band was so bad I just went back to my hotel and cried. That band couldn't read and they couldn't hear, either."[46]

His Own Band

The singer's management agency had always insisted that he could not afford a permanent band because he was not yet a big enough act. In 1954, however, the opportunity arose. Charles was hired to assemble a band to back singer Ruth Brown on a tour of Texas.

This was a seven-piece group—two trumpets, two saxes, plus piano, bass, and drums. (Unusually, there was no guitar.) The players were mostly rooted in funky, Texas-style blues and R&B, but they could also read complex jazz charts. Charles commented, "My theory was this: If I found cats who could play jazz, I could fix it so they could play my other little items—the rhythm-and-blues things. If a guy can handle jazz, that means he's a good musician, and it's easy for him to switch over to less complicated styles."[47]

When the tour with Brown ended, the core of the group remained together and Charles turned them into his first permanent band. Its cohesiveness, soulfulness, and sophistication were crucial to the next step in Charles's advancement. This began with an important audition in Atlanta, Georgia.

The singer wanted Ertegun and Wexler to hear the band perform several new songs he had worked up. (Abramson by now had left Atlantic.) Since his performing schedule would not bring him near New York, Charles asked the record executives to meet him at an Atlanta nightclub.

"I Knew Something Fantastic Had Happened"

The singer and his band were waiting, and when Ertegun and Wexler walked into the club Charles immediately counted off the first of several tunes. The record executives were stunned; Charles had clearly made a quantum leap since they had last heard him. Wexler recalled of the moment: "I knew something fantastic had happened. . . . Ray was full-fledged, ready for fame."[48]

One piece was especially exciting: the infectious "I Got a Woman," which Charles had cowritten with trumpeter Renald Richard. Ertegun and Wexler immediately arranged to record the song and rush it into production. It proved to be Charles's breakthrough record, speeding up the charts and peaking nationally at #15 on the R&B chart. It was far and away Charles's biggest hit to date.

"I Got a Woman" marked the beginning of a long string of smash hits for Charles. One of these was "This Little Girl of Mine," which—if not for Fats Domino's monster "Ain't It a Shame"—would have been Charles's first #1 hit on the R&B charts. This success did not go unnoticed in the press. For example, late in 1955, in the influential jazz magazine *Downbeat*, writer Ruth Cage devoted a column to the singer, noting that at age twenty-five "Ray Charles is on the threshold of a really great career."[49]

The Raelets

Not long after the success of "I Got a Woman," Charles refined the band's sound by adding vocalists. Charles loved playing off his voice against a group of female singers. He used a technique called call-and-response, which he borrowed directly from the black church tradition.

He first briefly hired a female singer, Mary Ann Fisher, featuring her in solo sets and as a backup vocalist. A more permanent arrangement, one that became crucial to Ray Charles's signature sound, was with a "girl group" of teenage vocalists hired for a recording session. These were the Cookies, led by Margie Hendricks, a singer with a distinctive growling style. Charles's first session with them produced several excellent songs, notably "Drown in My Own Tears." Soon, the Cookies were hired permanently, with their name changed to the Raelets. (The spelling has varied over the years.)

Spending a Little

Charles was making good money now. Nearly all his records were hits, and as his fame increased so did his fees for live dates. Furthermore, Elvis Presley recorded "I've Got a Woman" as the flip side of "Heartbreak Hotel," his first major-label single. Its skyrocketing popularity brought Charles substantial songwriting royalties.

The singer allowed himself to spend some of his money. Deciding to relocate to Los Angeles, he bought a house there for

In this photo from a 1963 performance, Ray Charles jams with a full band, which, in addition to his piano, featured drums, bass, guitar, and horns.

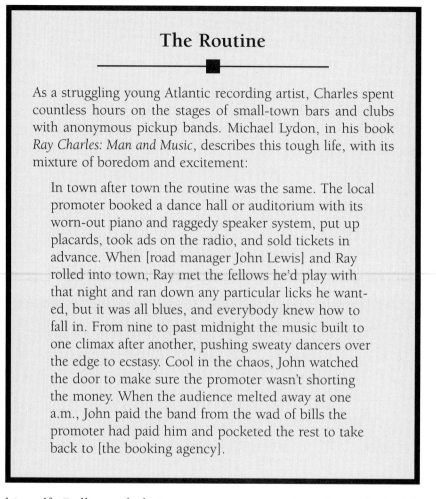

The Routine

As a struggling young Atlantic recording artist, Charles spent countless hours on the stages of small-town bars and clubs with anonymous pickup bands. Michael Lydon, in his book *Ray Charles: Man and Music*, describes this tough life, with its mixture of boredom and excitement:

> In town after town the routine was the same. The local promoter booked a dance hall or auditorium with its worn-out piano and raggedy speaker system, put up placards, took ads on the radio, and sold tickets in advance. When [road manager John Lewis] and Ray rolled into town, Ray met the fellows he'd play with that night and ran down any particular licks he wanted, but it was all blues, and everybody knew how to fall in. From nine to past midnight the music built to one climax after another, pushing sweaty dancers over the edge to ecstasy. Cool in the chaos, John watched the door to make sure the promoter wasn't shorting the money. When the audience melted away at one a.m., John paid the band from the wad of bills the promoter had paid him and pocketed the rest to take back to [the booking agency].

himself, Della, and their two young sons, Ray Jr. and David. Charles also bought himself new Cadillacs every year and replaced his band's aging station wagon.

The singer further invested in a relatively new invention: an electric piano. This freed him from having to use out-of-tune pianos on the road. "I often wouldn't play my trio numbers . . . because the pianos were so pathetic," he recalled. "I've seen some pretty incredible instruments, pianos so shoddy and flat that I had to play [in] C-sharp instead of C to be in the same key as the band."[50]

However, in general, Charles remained careful with his money and saved most of it. This frugality extended to paying his band. Charles's musicians were paid exactly what had been agreed, never a penny more or less. This was often lower than the pay in other bands, but it was offset for many musicians by the status and pleasure of playing with a challenging group.

Set for Stardom

By the end of the 1950s, Charles had come far. He was leading his own crackerjack band. He had released some twenty singles, fourteen of them substantial hits, as well as four long-playing albums. Furthermore, readers of *Downbeat* had just voted him the top new male singer and he was receiving significant recognition from European journalists.

Charles was also beginning to appeal to audiences beyond the relatively small confines of R&B. An all-jazz album was selling well, and his single "Swanee" was a hit on both the R&B and pop charts. This storming of two separate charts was a sign of a general breakdown of the barriers between traditionally separate musical styles.

Charles did not yet have the broad appeal of Elvis Presley, whose "Heartbreak Hotel" and "Blue Suede Shoes" both hit the #1 positions in the pop, country, *and* R&B charts. Charles was still popular primarily with black audiences, but his fan base was increasing. The stage was set for another major career shift—a period of innovation that would bring Charles unparalleled popularity.

Chapter Four

The Genius

Ray Charles is the only genius in our business.

—SINGER FRANK SINATRA
GIVING CHARLES HIS MOST FAMOUS NICKNAME

Throughout the 1950s, Charles had paid his dues as a hard-working musician. He had painstakingly refined his art, and he had enjoyed moderate success. During the next period of his life, however, Charles was more than moderately successful.

The singer was a music-industry phenomenon from the late 1950s into the mid-1960s; he knew exactly where he wanted to go, artistically as well as financially, and he had the will and the talent to get there. According to alto sax player Hank Crawford, the singer's longtime musical director and arranging partner, Charles's band members understood this well: "He was a *general!* And blind! He was young, but we followed him as an older person. He was striking a big chord with the world, and we felt it with him."[51]

Music fans already knew Charles through his rocking R&B hits, but that audience was relatively small compared to the overall music scene. Now, as Charles sought a vast new audience, his innovative work took some surprising turns and encompassed a wide range of classic American songs. These efforts were designed to keep him from being pigeonholed, music historian Richard Sudhalter notes: "Only by recording better-known standards was he going to transcend the R&B niche in which a category-conscious pop music industry had placed him."[52]

"What'd I Say"

In the summer of 1959, Charles sparked this period of intense creativity with an unrestrained, sexy, irresistible song called "What'd I Say." Opening with a catchy, repeated bass figure on an electric piano, "What'd I Say" was a perfect example of Charles's gift for merging two opposing but related forces—the frank sexuality of R&B and the fervent religious passion of gospel.

As the song progressed, Charles's singing evolved into a series of ecstatic moans and grunts, and the Raelets answered him in equally rapturous ways. This call-and-response precisely fused the Saturday night dance hall with Sunday morning church, as music historian Charlie Gillett points out: "The song [recreated] a revivalist meeting, with Charles declaring his love for woman instead of God but screaming, preaching, and haranguing his congregation in an otherwise authentic manner."[53]

According to legend, Charles spontaneously composed "What'd I Say" to fill time at the end of a Midwestern dance gig. Alternatively, it may have been carefully composed over a period of time, as many of Charles's songs were. In any case, Atlantic's executives loved it, recorded it quickly, and rushed it into stores.

Sales were disappointing at first. Record distributors complained that radio stations were avoiding it; the song was just too sexy. But a new version took off after Atlantic's engineer, Tom Dowd, edited the raciest parts out. The song shot to the #1 position on the R&B chart and reached #6 on the pop chart. "What'd I Say" became Charles's first monster hit and the first of his crossover hits—that is, songs that transcended genres like R&B or pop. Michael Lydon writes that it "became the life of a million parties, the spark of as many romances, [and] brought Ray Charles to everybody."[54]

Leaving Atlantic

"What'd I Say" was also one of Charles's last recordings for Atlantic. The label had nurtured and encouraged the singer, and he was deeply grateful to it. But Atlantic was still relatively small,

Mixing the Blues and Gospel

In this excerpt from his autobiography *Brother Ray*, the singer reflects on how his decision to mix gospel and blues freed him to develop his own distinctive style:

> Now, I'd been singing spirituals since I was three, and I'd been hearing the blues for just as long. These were my two main musical currents. So what could be more natural than to combine them? It didn't take any thinking, didn't take any calculating. All the sounds were there, right at the top of my head. . . . Nothing was more familiar to me, nothing more natural. Imitating Nat Cole had required a certain calculation on my part. . . . I loved doing it, but it certainly wasn't effortless. This new combination of blues and gospel was. It required nothing of me but being true to my very first music.

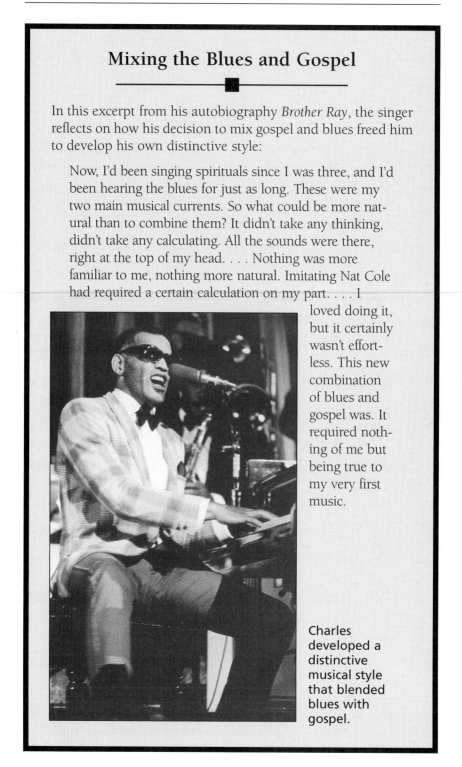

Charles developed a distinctive musical style that blended blues with gospel.

and it remained focused primarily on R&B; Charles had broader ambitions. His contract with Atlantic was due for renewal, and, despite Ertegun and Wexler's pleas to renew it, the singer was stalling them.

This was because his main contact at the Shaw Agency, Larry Myers, was urging him to consider other deals. Eager to expose Charles widely, Myers was booking him into venues that appealed to both white and black audiences. Myers reasoned that the singer also needed a bigger label—one that would not only encourage him to record diverse styles, but also have the resources to underwrite expensive studio recordings and distribute them widely.

Charles therefore pursued a deal with one of the industry's giants, ABC-Paramount Records. ABC (as it was known) was eager, offering the singer a better arrangement than Atlantic's for both advances (money paid before a recording is made) and royalties (a percentage of profits paid afterward). Even more important was ABC's guarantee that Charles would be his own producer. This meant not only full artistic freedom; it also meant a bigger slice of the financial pie.

"Either Way, He Was Gone"

For a record company to give an artist such power and freedom was unheard-of in an era when the record companies, not the musicians, held the power. But Charles wanted even more. He audaciously negotiated his right to own his own masters, the original recordings. Owning these meant that he would have the right to reissue his records in later years and receive all the profits.

ABC balked at first but eventually agreed that Charles could own his masters after five years. This gave the company a period in which to recoup its investment. The singer's lawyer urged him to take the deal, advising him that their offer was "the kind of contract even Sinatra doesn't get."[55]

Atlantic, with its modest resources, could not possibly match the offer. When Charles told them about it, Atlantic's executives felt betrayed; they had encouraged his talent and, they felt, understood him as no giant corporation ever could. Charles felt loyalty to Atlantic, but this was just too juicy a deal to turn down.

Memories differ on the sequence of events, but the end result was that Charles moved on. Jerry Wexler later commented, "Brother Ray and I have different memories of his departure. We frantically tried to chase him down, prepared to match any offer. We couldn't find him, couldn't get a meeting. Ray's version is that he sat down with Ahmet and was told Atlantic couldn't match the ABC money. Either way, he was gone, and so was my peace of mind."[56]

Just an Old, Sweet Song

Charles's first single for ABC, "My Baby," was disappointing, but his first long-playing record for the new company was dramatically different. *The Genius Hits the Road*, recorded in the spring of 1960, was a theme album; all the songs, drawn from mainstream American pop, were about places. Among them were classics like "Moonlight in Vermont," "California, Here I Come," and "Basin Street Blues."

The album's sound was a sharp departure from Charles's lean Atlantic recordings. The arrangements were lush and glossy, alternating between a string ensemble and a big band and with a full chorus frequently joining in. For the first time, Charles did not write his arrangements, beginning a tradition of ceding this part of the process to others.

One track on the album stood out: a sweetly yearning version of Hoagy Carmichael's 1930 tune "Georgia on My Mind." Charles outdid himself with this virtuoso performance, as writer Guy Martin notes: "Ray can round his voice out like a saxophone, or squeeze into a soft keening falsetto, or give it the punch and bite of a brass section, and in 'Georgia' he does all three."[57]

The song struck a responsive chord in audiences. It sold like wildfire, became the singer's first #1 pop single, and earned him his first Grammy award. Clearly, it represented just what Charles had hoped for—a new direction that could appeal to a broad and varied range of people.

More Mainstream Hits

Based on the success of *The Genius Hits the Road*, Charles's use of lush arrangements and mainstream pop standards—songs drawn from what is often called the Great American Songbook—was a

"Not As Dressed Up"

---◼---

Charles clearly saw the similarities between two seemingly diverse styles, country and R&B, and how they differed in common from the more sophisticated, Broadway-style songs from New York's Tin Pan Alley district. This quote by the singer is from Ben Fong-Torres's "The Rolling Stone Interview: Ray Charles" in *Rolling Stone* magazine:

> I think the words to country songs are very earthy like the blues, see, very down. They're not as dressed up, and the people are very honest and say, "Look, I miss you darlin', so I went out and I got drunk in a bar." Whereas Tin Pan Alley will say, "Oh, I missed you darling, so I went to this restaurant and I had dinner for one." That's cleaned up now, you see? But country songs and the blues is like it is.

winning formula. He stuck with it for his next project, *Dedicated to You*, an album of songs about one of his favorite subjects: women. Among its tunes were "Ruby," "Sweet Georgia Brown," and "Stella by Starlight."

Charles followed this album with a string of varied projects. One was *Genius + Soul = Jazz*, an all-jazz, mostly instrumental album with backing by the mighty Count Basie orchestra. Another was *Ray Charles and Betty Carter*, a collection of duets with an inventive, warm-voiced jazz singer.

Some fans and critics disliked Charles's new directions. They found the singer's take on mainstream pop bland and unexciting compared to his earlier recordings. There were rumors that he was being coerced, against his will, into recording this material. But the truth was simply that Charles liked all kinds of music, from lean R&B to the kind of schmaltzy pop that made purists cringe. No one ever forced him to record anything he disliked, he told a reporter: "If I like it, I don't give a damn what it is, I'll sing it. . . . Nobody told me to do 'Georgia' and nobody told me to do 'What'd I Say.' You know what I mean?"[58]

In 1961 Charles recorded a hit collection of duets with legendary jazz singer Betty Carter.

Many music reviewers—as well as his ever-broadening fan base—appreciated Charles's new directions. They felt that he was expanding his horizons without compromising. Typical of this attitude was *Downbeat* magazine's John Tynan. In a review of a concert that featured a big band, strings, and a chorus, Tynan noted, "Nothing in the music of this magnetic and profoundly moving musician has undergone change or cheapening. Nothing, in fact, has changed—except now the audience is larger."[59]

The Band Expands

Charles was clearly on a roll. His records were selling well, he was playing larger venues for bigger fees, and Tangerine, the music publishing company he had started, was thriving. The singer was getting rich.

Most of his money, as always, was saved or prudently invested, but he did spend some on luxuries. One was a Corvette sports car—he liked to shift the gears while someone else drove. A significant amount was reinvested in his music, particularly in hiring musicians. Since the singer now had the resources, he fulfilled a lifelong dream and put together a big band: the Ray Charles Orchestra, with sixteen top-notch musicians and four female singers in addition to the leader himself. Charles now had the roaring power of a big band behind him wherever he went.

Moving that many musicians around efficiently was a problem, however. Charles solved it by buying the first of several tour buses. Wanting to reach gigs faster and unwilling to endure the bus, he also bought the first of several airplanes. At this time, the early 1960s, it was rare for entertainers, especially black entertainers, to own their own planes; Charles may have been one of the first.

Building RPM

Charles formed his own record label during this period as well. Also called Tangerine, it was distributed by ABC. Charles used the Tangerine label to nurture and record other artists; the star himself still recorded for ABC.

Among the first artists signed to Tangerine was jazz singer Little Jimmy Scott, a diminutive man with an eerily androgynous voice. Blues singer Percy Mayfield was another early Tangerine artist. Mayfield, a gifted composer, was under contract to Charles as a songwriter; among the many hits he wrote for Charles was "Hit the Road, Jack," Charles's second #1 pop hit.

Charles also began building his own studio and office facilities, RPM International. (The initials stood for "recording, publishing, and management," but they also suggested the term used to indicate phonograph record speeds, "revolutions per minute.") Charles constructed a plain, windowless building in a nondescript block of South Central Los Angeles, renting the first floor out and using the second for his own purposes. Writer Guy Martin noted that the building's dull exterior hid the creative ferment inside: "The place looks more like an intelligence garrison or a small fort than a house of music."[60]

Joe Adams

A growing number of employees ensured that Charles's enterprises ran smoothly. Among them was a succession of personal

Joe Adams accepts a Grammy award in 2005. Adams was one of Ray Charles's most trusted financial advisors.

valets, who ran errands and helped the singer with chores that he could not do himself. He also relied on a series of music directors and road managers, who made sure that things ran smoothly on the band's hectic, nearly nonstop tours.

But Charles's only really close associate was Joe Adams. Adams was a dapper, imperious former disc jockey who had advanced in Charles's organization from announcer to business manager and partner. Charles admired Adams's financial acumen; Adams had already been well off when he went to work for the singer. Adams advised his boss on the formation and design of the RPM building, as well as on such investments as apartment houses, a ranch, and a travel agency. Adams also helped Charles build a palatial house, complete with piano-shaped pool, in the exclusive Baldwin Hills neighborhood of Los Angeles. (Charles's family needed the room now that it was augmented by a third son, Robert.)

In Joe Adams, Charles had one trusted assistant he could rely on, rather than having to deal directly with many different employees; Adams served as a hard-nosed buffer between the singer and everyone else. But Charles, habitually mistrustful of others, was wary even of Adams's help. Charles used RPM's secretary, Ethel Rubin, as a watchdog in the office, making sure that Adams never overstepped his bounds or took advantage.

Working

Once Charles's business headquarters and day-to-day business operations were established, the singer settled into a regular schedule: touring from late spring into the winter, then spending the early part of the new year in Los Angeles recording the next album.

A lifelong workaholic and perfectionist, Charles habitually spent long hours in the RPM building; one associate estimated that Charles spent ten hours as a businessman for every hour he spent as an entertainer. Often, the singer did not get home until dawn. And then there was the relentless touring; starting in 1961, his schedule was stepped up even further to include overseas dates.

From the beginning, his European dates had been triumphs; jazz and R&B fans there, given a rare chance to hear their idol in those days when world tours were rare, reacted to him ecstatically. Journalist Thomas Thompson wrote that Charles's first shows in Paris "were sold out within hours after they were announced and were attended by worshipers who flew in from Rome and Stockholm and Berlin."[61]

Touring in America

Touring in America, in sharp contrast, was much more difficult. At the height of the civil rights movement in America in the late 1950s and early 1960s, a traveling black musician moved in a volatile atmosphere, especially in the segregated South. Despite his prominence, Charles and his band members were subjected to discrimination and even outright hostility.

The singer had never been outspoken about segregation, preferring to keep his opinions to himself. His longtime tenor saxophonist, David "Fathead" Newman, recalled being on the road in the 1950s with the singer: "Ray didn't say much about [segregation]; the only thing about it he would rebel against was when we'd stop to get gas. He would be filling up all of our vehicles, and if they wouldn't allow him to use the restroom, he'd tell them to stop pumping the gas right away."[62]

But in the spring of 1961, in the midst of the civil right movement, the singer made a rare public statement. Charles was scheduled to play a dance in Augusta, Georgia; as was customary there, black and white audience members would be kept separate. But when Augusta's student activists challenged Charles to do something about the situation, he announced he would not play to a segregated audience.

When the promoter refused to alter his plans, the singer left town without performing. The promoter sued, and in time Charles paid $757 in fines. Civil rights activists across the country applauded his action; the response of one African American newspaper, the *Pittsburgh Courier*, was typical: "America's Great High Priest of Jazz dealt his [birth] state's racial bias a resounding slap in the face."[63]

"Then, Boom, It Worked"

An even stronger statement by Charles about racial division, and the elusive promise of unity, came not with a formal protest but in the guise of music—specifically, an album of country music. Today, this might not seem especially amazing or unusual,

Charles celebrates after a 1981 performance in Paris, where, throughout his career, he played to sold-out crowds.

but it was a powerful and startling venture in 1962, when country music was considered a "white" genre. The idea that a black man could sing country music—and do so brilliantly—was a shock.

The album, *Modern Sounds in Country and Western Music*, was made up of solid, familiar country hits like Hank Williams's "Hey, Good Lookin'" and Eddy Arnold's "You Don't Know Me." Chosen for their heartfelt, universally appealing lyrics, these well-known songs were radically altered by Charles, given the lavish string/big band/chorus treatment that had worked for him in the past. The result upended everyone's preconceptions while revealing some striking similarities in spirit between R&B and country. The album could thus be seen as brilliant entertainment, a sly political statement, or both.

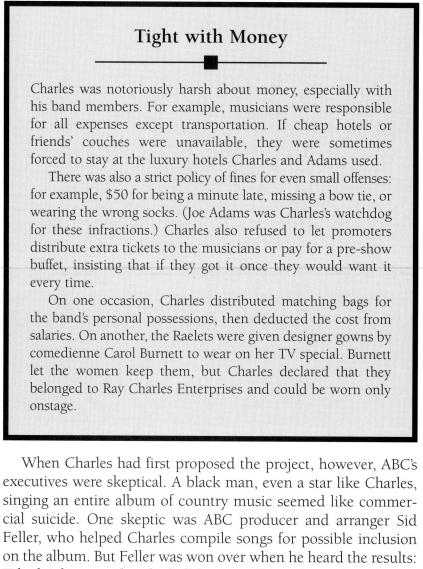

Tight with Money

Charles was notoriously harsh about money, especially with his band members. For example, musicians were responsible for all expenses except transportation. If cheap hotels or friends' couches were unavailable, they were sometimes forced to stay at the luxury hotels Charles and Adams used.

There was also a strict policy of fines for even small offenses: for example, $50 for being a minute late, missing a bow tie, or wearing the wrong socks. (Joe Adams was Charles's watchdog for these infractions.) Charles also refused to let promoters distribute extra tickets to the musicians or pay for a pre-show buffet, insisting that if they got it once they would want it every time.

On one occasion, Charles distributed matching bags for the band's personal possessions, then deducted the cost from salaries. On another, the Raelets were given designer gowns by comedienne Carol Burnett to wear on her TV special. Burnett let the women keep them, but Charles declared that they belonged to Ray Charles Enterprises and could be worn only onstage.

When Charles had first proposed the project, however, ABC's executives were skeptical. A black man, even a star like Charles, singing an entire album of country music seemed like commercial suicide. One skeptic was ABC producer and arranger Sid Feller, who helped Charles compile songs for possible inclusion on the album. But Feller was won over when he heard the results: "I hadn't known what the hell he was talking about, then, boom, it worked. Ray understood country music. He loved the simple plaintive lyrics, and he felt that giving the music a lush treatment would make it different."[64]

"I Can't Stop Loving You"

Once again, Charles's instincts were right. *Modern Sounds* was a favorite of critics and radio disc jockeys everywhere and a smash hit. It stayed at the #1 position on the album charts for fourteen weeks and remained on the charts for a total of two years, becoming ABC's first million-selling album.

One song in particular, Don Gibson's "I Can't Stop Loving You," surprised everyone. Charles had not initially considered it as a single, but radio disc jockeys reported that listeners wanted to buy it. The song was trimmed to single length (the vinyl singles then used could not be more than about three minutes in length), shot to the #1 spot on the pop charts, and stayed there for five weeks in the summer of 1962. It also topped the R&B and easy listening charts—but not, oddly, the country charts. This unexpected success was a phenomenon that happens only a few times in a decade—a hit that comes from nowhere to surprise even canny veterans like Charles.

Thanks to the country album and the singer's other successes of the late 1950s and early 1960s, Ray Charles was now one of the most popular figures in music. Only Elvis Presley, Fats Domino, and Frank Sinatra rivaled him—at least in those days before the Beatles invaded. However, Charles was about to hit a rough patch in his personal life; his ability to survive and to keep on creating was about to be severely tested.

Chapter Five

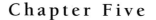

A Rough Patch for the Genius

Ray is the earth. —JAZZ DRUMMER CHICO HAMILTON

The rough patch Charles hit was caused by his drug addiction. For years the singer had prided himself on his self-control, claiming that his heroin use was never bad enough to affect his performance. This assertion has been backed up by others, including Atlantic's Jerry Wexler: "There wasn't an instance when his addiction interfered with his work. . . . When it came to Ray's professionalism, there could be no grounds for complaint. He worked his ass off."[65]

Now, however, perhaps because Charles's wealth gave him access to more and better drugs, the heroin was getting out of control. He started occasionally missing gigs because he was high, something that had never happened in his early days. His drug use also caused a serious accident when Charles cut an artery and tendon in his hand on a glass table while high at home. Unable to seek help himself, the singer probably would have bled to death if his young son had not discovered him in time.

Early Arrests
Early in his career, Charles had had a few brushes with the law over drugs. These included a 1955 arrest in Philadelphia, Penn-

sylvania, when police raided the singer's dressing room and arrested him and several band members. Charles's lawyer learned that the charges would disappear in exchange for a $6,000 fine. The singer paid what amounted to a bribe, but the episode confirmed his already cynical view of the legal system.

Charles was busted twice more in 1961. He spent several hours in jail in Chicago, Illinois, but the charges were dismissed because he had been illegally searched. An arrest in Indianapolis, Indiana, also resulted in dropped charges, because the police had used a ruse to enter Charles's dressing room without a warrant.

The Indiana bust was widely publicized, and in its wake a number of important gigs disappeared. Ed Sullivan, host of the

In 1961 Indianapolis detectives arrest Ray Charles for possession of narcotics. The charges were later dropped.

nation's most popular television variety show, canceled an upcoming appearance by Charles. Other promoters, fearing a no-show or reluctant to be associated with the singer, likewise declined to book him.

The Boston Bust

These arrests were relatively minor compared to the events of October 1964, when Charles's jet landed in Boston from Canada. (This was a passenger jet the singer had purchased to carry the whole band.) After checking into his hotel, Charles realized that his drugs were still on the plane. Not trusting others to carry them, he and his chauffeur returned to the airport.

Federal customs officers, aware of Charles's reputation, observed the two enter the plane. When they emerged, agents detained them. Disbelieving Charles's explanation that he had gone to get a book, they searched his overcoat and found marijuana, heroin, and "works"—equipment for cooking and shooting up heroin.

The singer was released on bail and performed that night, but the situation was dire. Customs officers had found more drugs on the plane. Also, since he had arrived from Canada, Charles faced charges of smuggling as well as narcotics possession. He was looking at a potential sixty years in jail and $40,000 in fines. Furthermore, his plane was impounded, which severely limited Charles's ability to travel and work.

In the Hospital

Charles canceled all public appearances indefinitely. He knew that without touring he risked losing his audience, but he felt it was more important to concentrate on tasks at home. He needed to deal with his legal situation, and he wanted to take care of business affairs such as finishing the new RPM studio.

In February 1965, a federal grand jury formally charged Charles with possession and smuggling of narcotics. The singer by then had decided on a strategy. He thought that the best way to bolster his case was to kick heroin; judges tended to look favorably on sincere efforts by addicts to clean themselves up.

Charles felt strong enough, mentally and physically, to go cold turkey—to quit using heroin all at once, without other drugs to

Ray Charles plays chess on a specially-designed board. Charles developed a fondness for chess while he was in the hospital seeking treatment for his heroin addiction.

ease the transition. He hired a prominent psychiatrist, Dr. Frederick Hacker, to help him through the process and in July entered St. Francis Hospital in suburban Lynwood, California. Officially, the singer was being treated for depression and overwork.

Heroin withdrawal is an ugly business. For two days Charles did little but vomit, shake, and sweat. On the third and fourth days, he was weak but able to eat a little. After that, as he gained strength, his hospital stay settled into a routine. Afternoons were for dozing, nights for pacing and thinking about the future, and mornings for visits with others. Della brought him food, nurses played cards with him, and Hacker taught him chess.

This game quickly became an important part of Charles's life. At first he lost every time, but he was a quick learner and boasted that he never lost the same way twice. Chess appealed to his competitive nature, to his ability to visualize complex structures in his head, and to his analytical powers. Charles also loved it because no luck was involved. He once remarked, "With cards, no matter how well you play, you ain't gonna win unless the cards fall for you. But in chess, *it's my brain against yours!*"[66]

The End of the Heroin Years

Within weeks, Charles was calling his office to discuss business with Joe Adams (who had been running the office in his boss's absence). He was soon allowed to leave the hospital for short periods. He was discharged in October and pled guilty at the trial date the following month.

The singer admitted during the trial to previous trouble over narcotics. However, his lawyers argued that this time, unlike his previous arrests, he had freed himself of heroin and intended to stay clean. Defense attorney Paul J. Redmond stated that Charles "has great confidence in the people he has been working with, and that they have set out a program that [will] greatly aid him in staying off narcotics."[67]

The government acknowledged that Charles was clean and that he was a man of strong willpower with the ability to stay off drugs permanently. Nonetheless, arguing that he should not be allowed to go unpunished, prosecutors suggested two years in prison and a $10,000 fine. The judge held off on sentencing for a year, ordering the singer to report periodically to court-authorized doctors for testing. Charles passed these tests over the next year and was given a $10,000 fine and a suspended sentence.

Back on the Block

After the sentencing was delayed, Charles could resume his normal life and immediately began touring again. The singer recovered his airplane from customs and revived his band, this time making sure that everyone was clean of drugs. He wanted no chance of more trouble.

Worried that the public might avoid Charles because of the stigma of drugs, Adams hired a public relations firm to boost the singer's public image. This campaign resulted in, among other things, a positive profile in *Life* magazine—a seal of approval from America's premier magazine. Also, Los Angeles city councilman (later mayor) Tom Bradley declared a "Ray Charles Day" for the city.

Meanwhile, Charles's personal life seemed to improve without drugs. The singer claimed that he never noticed a big difference in his health or personal manner after quitting heroin; the only change, he said, was that he did not crave a fix every day. However, Charles's valet at the time, Vernon Troupe, disagreed: "There had been something pitiful about Ray when he got stoned. It was like being with a stranger. He knew me but only as my function, a tool that got him from one place to another. The warmth that I got afterward, the kidding and joking, the *person*, were not there in the heroin days."[68]

Challengers

But Charles was worried about more than simply having the public shun him over the drug issue. A year out of the public eye can be an eternity in the rapidly changing world of popular music. The music scene of the mid-1960s, moreover, was especially volatile. A new style, rock and roll, was starting to dominate the music charts, and a new generation of singers was challenging established artists like Charles.

A watershed moment in this change had occurred early in 1964, when American music fans embraced four young musicians

"I Did It and It's Done"

Charles always maintained that it was his own decision to use drugs and his own strength of will that enabled him to stop. He never condoned drug use, but he also fiercely believed it was private business, as he told writer Whitney Balliett in *American Singers:*

> What I did is done and that's that. I've been talking about drugs to the papers and everybody for a long time, and I could continue to talk about it for thirty more years. But if you make a mistake and rectify it, you don't want to hear about it for the rest of your life. I'm no missionary or pope and I'm not trying to reform anybody. I did it and it's done and over and that's that.

from England, the Beatles, with something close to mass hysteria. This phenomenon, an event the press dubbed Beatlemania, transformed American pop music; it opened the floodgates for an army of bands from England—the so-called British Invasion—and cemented rock and roll's place at the top of the pops.

Rock and roll was deeply influenced by the R&B singers of the 1950s; as a result, Ray Charles was a hero to many rockers. Paul McCartney, for one, has commented often about the excitement he felt on hearing "What'd I Say" as an English schoolboy. It was a major factor in his decision to take up music.

Nonetheless, for older singers like Charles, the arrival of rock and roll was not good news. It was music for young people, and these teenagers were now the ones buying records in huge numbers—not their parents. Charles, once the superstar of ABC Records, was not even the label's top seller any more, that position having been usurped by a California pop group, the Mamas and the Papas. As the singer prepared his return to the music scene, it seemed entirely possible that—still in his early thirties— he might have already peaked.

That Sweet Soul Music

Charles need not have worried; the public had not forgotten him. The singer's first tours were tremendous successes; he performed to capacity audiences, and critics noted that he played and sang wonderfully. The first recordings he released during his comeback were also gratifying successes.

Charles had started preparing a new album even before his trial. This record, *Crying Time*, shrewdly used elements of both

Charles performs with the Raelets during a 1960s concert. Despite the rising popularity of rock and roll in the 1960s, Charles's appeal remained as strong as ever.

the funky, horn-driven R&B of his Atlantic hits and the glossy sophistication of his ABC recordings. Contrary to Charles's fears, it sold extremely well and spawned two hit singles: "Let's Go Get Stoned" (the defiant title ostensibly referred to drinking, not drugs) and "Crying Time," Charles's plaintive version of a hit for country star Buck Owens.

During this period, Charles also received recognition for his role in shaping a new and exciting form that black pop music was taking—a deeply influential style called soul. Though it took many forms, soul could be characterized as the next generation of rhythm and blues. It forged the rocking beat of R&B with passionate vocals from the gospel tradition and added high-powered, sophisticated instrumental work that owed a debt to both jazz and pop music.

Singers like Aretha Franklin, Sam Cooke, and James Brown epitomized this fiery new sound. Several record labels also put their distinctive stamps on it; among the most prominent were Motown (whose groups included the Miracles, the Supremes, and the Four Tops) and Stax/Volt (whose artists included Otis Redding, Carla Thomas, and Wilson Pickett).

Every soul singer had a distinctive style, and there were countless variations on the basic sound and countless giants of the genre. However, it was widely acknowledged that Ray Charles was soul music's chief pioneer. Soul might have come into being without him, but it would have sounded radically different; according to Joe Levy of *Rolling Stone* magazine, "The hit records [Charles] made for Atlantic in the mid-50s mapped out everything that would happen to . . . soul music in the years that followed."[69]

Charles' trailblazing fusion of R&B and gospel had created a sturdy framework for virtually every future variation; in short, he was singing soul music years before the term was coined. "What'd I Say" may not have been the first soul song, but it was certainly a basic template on which countless others were modeled. Music critic Henry Pleasants summed up Charles's contribution by commenting, "Ray Charles [was] to soul what Louis Armstrong was to jazz—the herald of a new style."[70]

The Seventies

The recognition Charles received for his pioneering of soul music and the success of his recordings after his year off buoyed him and kept him in the public eye. Nonetheless, the changes wrought by the shifting music scene were inevitable. *Crying Time* proved to be Charles's last album to crack the Top Forty, and the single of "Crying Time" was his last to be a Top Ten pop hit. As

"America"

As Michael Lydon points out in this excerpt from *Ray Charles: Man and Music*, the singer's definitive version of "America the Beautiful" summarized his own musical journey and seemed to represent all Americans as no other version had before it:

> "America" had grown from an overlooked album track into an anthem that conveyed to millions a rugged, determined love of the country and its highest ideals. In responding to Ray singing "America," listeners implicitly recognized that after forty years of crisscrossing the land and playing songs from every native idiom, Ray Charles had reached his goal, the heart of American music. Singing from the heart, Ray had found a way to speak soul-to-soul with Americans of every creed and color.

Ray Charles performs his unique rendition of "America the Beautiful" before the second game of the 2001 World Series in Phoenix.

the 1960s moved into the 1970s, the singer's glory years—his days of dominating the music scene—were fading.

Charles did make some memorable records in the 1970s. For example, he collaborated with British singer Cleo Laine on a robust version of *Porgy and Bess*, George Gershwin's "folk opera." Also, his moving—some say definitive—interpretation of "America the Beautiful" was a surprise hit during the country's bicentennial celebrations in 1976. And Charles made a memorable guest appearance on Aretha Franklin's *Live at the Fillmore* album when the two sang together on "Spirit in the Dark." Charles did not know the song when Aretha called him on stage to sing it— but he faked it admirably, and the results were electrifying.

However, notable recordings were exceptions. Most fans and critics were disappointed by Charles's 1970s albums, finding them bland and mediocre. Music historian Charlie Gillett commented that the singer "degenerated [in] a musical decline closely matching that of Elvis Presley. Charles applied his style to anything, inevitably adjusting himself to awkward material, losing contact with the cultural roots that had inspired his style."[71]

Disappointing Sales

Sales of these records were so poor, in fact, that ABC did not renew Charles's contract. He promptly started a new company, Crossover, which was distributed by London Records. The singer's first Crossover release, *Come Live with Me*, was a credible mix of country and R&B, but it sold poorly. Not counting instrumental jazz, it was the first Ray Charles album since the 1950s to miss being on the charts altogether.

An exception to his generally mediocre records in the 1970s was an album distributed by Charles's old label, Atlantic, which had thrived under the guidance of producer Ahmet Ertegun. This record, *True to Life*, was a notable success—thanks in part to Atlantic's powerful distribution system but also because it contained more popular selections, including the Beatles' "Let It Be," Louisiana rocker Bobby Charles's "Jealous Kind," and older standards like "Oh, What a Beautiful Morning."

Despite generally poor sales, Charles resisted pressure—as he had all through his career—to record in currently fashionable musical styles. He insisted on playing only songs he liked and only in his own way. Over and over, he stated his belief that no one could predict what would be a hit; he simply recorded what moved him.

On the Road

His record sales may have declined, but Charles remained a popular concert draw. Throughout the 1970s, Charles continued to tour relentlessly. Long after the era of the touring big bands, the Ray Charles Orchestra was still going strong. Writer Guy Martin, profiling the singer, noted Charles's insatiable appetite for the road: "He consumes the road, he slides down it like it is a smooth walnut banister. It bothers him so little that in the States, if there is a day between shows, he flies to the soul bunker [the RPM building] for a little office work and then back to the next gig, crossing the country twice in as many days."[72]

On the road, as had been the case for years, the singer's routine was unvarying. In part this was simply because of his blindness; Charles naturally preferred familiar surroundings. For example, he checked into the same suite in the same hotel in a given city whenever possible; he especially liked Holiday Inns, because their floor plans were usually laid out in similar ways.

If faced with an unfamiliar hotel suite, Charles got to know it through music. He took small steps around while whistling a tune. This measured the room for him: so many bars of music to the bathroom in one direction, so many to the phone in another.

Other preperformance rituals also remained unchanged. Charles liked to read detective novels in his hotel suite, and he always ate there as well. As showtime neared, a valet helped Charles dress and get to the performance hall. The singer then relaxed backstage, smoking and drinking coffee laced with sugar and gin. He apparently never got seriously drunk on this "Ray Charles cocktail," but it was a constant companion.

Shortly before showtime, Charles dictated a set list—a list of songs to be played that night—to his musical director. (Out of some 250 songs in the band's "book," about 60 would be well rehearsed and ready at any given time.) The musical director, in turn, passed the list out to the band.

On stage, the band had to watch the leader carefully. Charles conducted using his whole body; he kept time by rocking his

On Stage and in Motion

This description of a typical Ray Charles performance is from writer Guy Martin's 1986 *Esquire* magazine article "Blue Genius":

> He's perched right on a corner of his black leather and brass stool, his legs spread, his arms stretched in the attack. He holds his back straight as he swings from side to side, a metronome running on funk. Every part of his body moves to a different part of the music, but his feet provide the most deft, airborne accompaniment. His black patent-leather pumps flash around the legs of his stool like shiny blackbirds feeding: they give us the backbeat, the downbeat, the accents, the tempo. One is quickly aware that Ray conducts this way, that his entire band, while appearing to read the charts, actually watches the man's feet. Ray kicks the song in the air like a seal slapping a beach ball and then jumps up as if he's just received a few hundred volts from his stool for the stiff-backed, duck-walk-the-keyboard finale.

Throughout his career, Charles performed seated before his piano on a black leather and brass stool.

Ray Charles, his wife Della, and their sons take a walk outside their Los Angeles home in 1966. Charles and his wife divorced in 1977.

torso, and he used other physical cues as well. The bass player stood near Charles and could see his feet, which the singer used to signal changes, such as slowing down the end of a tune or adding an extra chorus. It was the bassist's responsibility to watch Charles's feet and pass the cues on. And woe to any musician who missed a cue; a salty lecture after the show was certain and sometimes a fine as well. Bassist Jimmy Bell recalled, "I learned that with Ray, the music's gonna be right or not at all. Off the bandstand he's nice, but on the stand he's a horse of a different color."[73]

End of a Marriage

During the 1970s, Charles endured a major change in his personal life: his marriage to Della ended. The singer had always been a poor family man, refusing to hide his multiple affairs and remaining cold to his children (those he had with other women as well as those with Della). Della had tolerated this, as well as the drug use, for years; Charles wrote in his autobiography, "I give her a great deal of credit for putting up with me and my strange ways."[74]

By the mid-1970s, however, she was unwilling to tolerate the relationship on these terms. The couple separated, with the singer living in the RPM building or in a series of apartments. Della filed for divorce in May 1976, and it was finalized at the end of 1977. In the financial settlement, she got the house, her car, and a trust fund for all the boys, as well as a considerable cash payment and monthly support for the two boys still at home. Everything else, including all of the business ventures and properties, remained in Charles's name.

The divorce was just one aspect of the unstable nature of the decade for Charles. The hit records were no longer coming, and, as the 1980s dawned, he found that even his longtime ace in the hole—his popularity as a concert draw—was uncertain. In the next and last period of his life, Charles was forced to invent new ways to stay fresh and alive for the public, but he also began to reap the considerable benefits of being an elder statesman of music.

Chapter Six

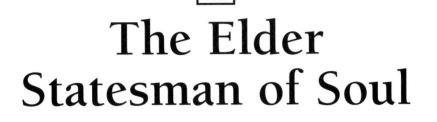

The Elder Statesman of Soul

A true artist will be around for a long time. That's the way I look at it.

—RAY CHARLES

I never wanted to be famous, but I always wanted to be great.

—RAY CHARLES

As Charles moved into his fifties, his longtime audience base was aging along with him. He found that fans were less willing to go out at night to see performers like him, and the kind of club popular with singers of his generation was consequently going out of style. Shockingly, Charles's live shows sometimes failed to sell well. He was forced to downsize his schedule accordingly, with each year's tour periods shrinking from nine months to six or less.

Live shows were Charles's lifeblood, so this was disheartening news. Fortunately, he was able to cultivate some fertile new performance outlets. One involved extended bookings in Las Vegas casinos. These gigs were good because the pay was excellent and travel was minimal.

Symphonies

Another outlet involved appearances with classical symphony orchestras. The idea of performing with full symphonic backing was not new to the singer; in the past, he had made occasional appearances with the Los Angeles Philharmonic and similar organizations. Now, however, Charles began to focus on these gigs, connecting with orchestras around the world at every opportunity.

These symphonic appearances were financially rewarding; fees were high and expenses low. The main work was complete once Sid Feller, the singer's friend since his days at ABC, rewrote the band's music charts into full symphonic scores. Logistical problems were also minimized; the Charles organization needed to supply only a handful of people—primarily the singer himself and Feller (who conducted), plus Charles's regular guitarist,

Ray Charles performs with an orchestra at the 2003 Montreal Jazz Festival. Charles did many such performances in his later years.

bassist, and drummer. Furthermore, rehearsals were a snap, since classical musicians sight-read fluently.

Orchestral gigs were also artistically rewarding. They allowed Charles to re-create, live and onstage, a musical atmosphere he loved: the plush, woodwinds-and-strings sound he had used in the studio with great success. Orchestral gigs were also satisfying for Charles because he enjoyed appearing onstage with highly trained classical musicians and was never intimidated or fazed by them: "The feelings, the grooves, *are* different. You can't turn a jazz band into a symphony or a symphony into a jazz band. But I'm a *musician*, and whatever I'm playing, country, blues, jazz, or classical, I adapt myself to the mode that I'm dealing with at the time."[75]

"Everybody Knew Ray"

In addition to concert appearances, Charles maintained a prominent place in the public's eye during this period by making cameos, often nonmusical, in movies and on television. On TV, for example, he appeared as himself on the children's show *Sesame Street* and on the situation comedy *Who's the Boss?* He also appeared on *Saturday Night Live* as both host and musical guest.

Some of Charles's highest-profile nonmusical appearances came in commercials for Diet Pepsi. (Earlier, he had done a series of radio ads for Pepsi's rival, Coca-Cola!) The immensely popular Pepsi ads featured a trio of women known as the "Uh-Huh Girls"—a spin on the ads' catch-phrase "You got the right one, baby, uh-huh!" The ads played off Charles's blindness, as in one in which an offscreen person tries to switch Charles's can of Diet Pepsi for a Coke—but fails to fool him.

Charles's film appearances likewise made good-natured fun of his blindness. One example was his turn in the spoof *Spy Hard*. The singer's role as a bus driver was small but memorable: he turned around as a pretty girl got on the bus, grinned, and said "Nice dress!" before pulling out into traffic.

The apex of Charles's movie career was as a gun-toting pawnshop owner in *The Blues Brothers*, which starred comics John Belushi and Dan Aykroyd as blues-obsessed siblings. (Charles sang a rousing version of "Shake a Tail Feather" in the movie.) *The Blues Brothers* was wildly successful and served as a huge boost to the careers of Charles and fellow guest stars Aretha Franklin and

James Brown, introducing them to millions of new listeners and reminding old ones that they were still electrifying performers.

Thanks to such high-profile appearances, Charles was recognized even more than before; in public places, children sometimes recognized him before their parents did. One of the singer's valets, Dave Simmons, recalls, "Kids knew him from *Sesame Street*, black folks knew him from the blues, and the white folks knew him from all the country-and-western. Everybody knew Ray, everywhere in the world."[76]

Recordings

Charles's appearances in the movies and elsewhere were necessary because his recordings continued to disappoint, both artistically and financially. At one point, he was unable to secure a distribution contract and, for the first time in sixteen years, did not make an album during his off-season from touring.

This drought did not last long, and Charles did make some notable recordings during the 1980s and '90s. In 1985, for example, he participated in "We Are the World," an all-star benefit recording to aid African hunger programs. This was a rare instance of Ray Charles singing for free; the singer disliked benefits, but made an exception for one of the event's organizers, his old friend Quincy Jones.

Other noteworthy recordings during this time included a guest appearance on Jones's *Back on the Block* album, with Charles singing a joyful version of his old hit "Let the Good Times Roll." The singer also received his eleventh Grammy award in 1990 for "I'll Be Good to You," a spirited duet with singer Chaka Khan. In addition, Charles recorded "Baby Grand," a charming duet with pianist-singer-songwriter Billy Joel, who wrote the song specifically for Charles. Joel's memories of the experience are strong:

> When he walked into that session, it was like the Washington Monument just walked in the room. He looked exactly like Ray Charles was supposed to look: He had the glasses, the hair and the smile. He was tough, though. If the drummer dropped the beat, he could be scary as crap. You didn't want to make a mistake around Ray Charles, because you could feel this glare coming from somewhere behind those glasses.[77]

"It Was All Music to Ray"

———————■———————

Ray Charles had a profound impact on generations of musicians. Among the many rock and roll musicians who paid tribute to him at the time of his death was Keith Richards of the Rolling Stones. This quote is from the article "Remembering Ray" in *Rolling Stone* magazine: "The man had range. He wasn't in a bag. He had his own bag. I loved the way he could effortlessly zoom about in all of these things. It was all music to Ray. He was the first true crossover artist. . . . Ray was rock & roll. He was rhythm & blues. He was jazz. He was country. He had such reach—and far-reaching effect."

Back to the Country

But the major success of Charles's recordings during this period involved a return to country music. The singer had done a few country-oriented projects since the glory days of the 1960s. Among these were a guest spot on the variety TV show *Hee Haw*, a duet with actor Clint Eastwood for the movie *Any Which Way You Can*, and an appearance at the Grand Ole Opry with singer Loretta Lynn.

The country audiences had welcomed Charles warmly, perhaps because they tended to be more accepting of older performers than pop-music fans. Buoyed by this response, Charles planned a return visit to the genre; CBS Records' Nashville division took a chance on signing him despite his uneven sales figures in recent years.

The first of Charles's CBS albums, *Wish You Were Here Tonight*, was recorded mostly at RPM Studios, with overdubs by Nashville studio musicians. Critics mostly panned it, but audiences loved it. The album sold well, and soon after its release Charles was honored with top billing at the Country Music Association's twenty-fifth anniversary concert in Washington, D.C., with President and Mrs. Reagan in attendance. Pleased, the singer quickly recorded two more country albums, *Do I Ever Cross Your Mind?* and *From the Pages of My Mind*.

Ray Charles and country star Willie Nelson rehearse a duet. Charles recorded several duets with country music stars.

He also teamed up with a veteran Nashville producer, Billy Sherrill, to record *Friendship*, an album of duets with such country legends as George Jones, Hank Williams Jr., Merle Haggard, and Willie Nelson. Unlike the process commonly used on other celebrity duet albums, where vocals are recorded at different times and places, Charles insisted on singing live with his partners. This gave the album an especially warm, personal feel, and fans responded by making it a #1 hit on the country charts.

Honors, Awards, Donations

Acceptance from country music fans was not the only honor awarded to Charles. He had long been a legendary figure, a beloved icon and a true elder statesman of American music, and toward the end of his life the honors and awards began pouring in.

These honors had actually begun long before, when the singer had started racking up Grammy awards and gold records. They continued when the city council of Los Angeles had proclaimed "Ray Charles Day." Then, in 1979, the Georgia House of Representatives made the singer's version of "Georgia on My Mind" the official state song and invited him to sing it at the capitol in Atlanta.

In the 1980s, however, the accolades really began to roll in. Among them was a Kennedy Center Honor, America's most distinguished award for the arts. Charles was given the National Medal of Arts as well. The French government similarly honored him, giving him the title of Commander of Fine Arts and Letters.

The singer was one of the first musicians inducted into the Rock and Roll Hall of Fame. Induction into several other honored groups followed, including the Jazz, Songwriters', Florida Artists, Georgia Music, and Rhythm & Blues Halls of Fame. Then there were Grammy awards (twelve in all, including one for Lifetime Achievement), plus three Emmy nominations and a star on the Hollywood Walk of Fame.

Charles also received honorary doctorates from a number of universities. These were given in honor of his achievements as a pioneering African American musician and businessman and often as well in recognition of generous donations he made to the schools. Florida A&M in Tallahassee was the first such institution to honor him this way. Other colleges and universities followed,

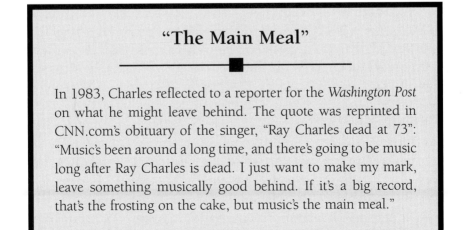

"The Main Meal"

In 1983, Charles reflected to a reporter for the *Washington Post* on what he might leave behind. The quote was reprinted in CNN.com's obituary of the singer, "Ray Charles dead at 73": "Music's been around a long time, and there's going to be music long after Ray Charles is dead. I just want to make my mark, leave something musically good behind. If it's a big record, that's the frosting on the cake, but music's the main meal."

including Occidental, Morehouse, Dillard, Wilberforce, Albany (Georgia) State, and the University of South Florida.

In addition to donating large sums to colleges and universities, Charles distributed his wealth to several other worthy causes. One of these was medical research. In 1983, the singer had a problem with one ear. Doctors treated it successfully, but the prospect of deafness terrified him. In response, he created the Robinson Foundation for Hearing Disorders, which had a special focus on creating devices to help the congenitally deaf.

"Brother Ray, You've Been a Good Horse"

With age Charles began to suffer physical ailments even more serious than his hearing difficulties. One was a bad hip that required replacement surgery in 2003. As he was being treated for this, doctors discovered an even more serious illness: The singer's liver was failing.

Charles, on tour when his liver problem was diagnosed, was forced to cancel his remaining performances. With the exception of his year off while kicking heroin, it was the first time in fifty-three consecutive years that he had had to cancel a tour. "It breaks my heart to withdraw from these shows," he said at the time. "All my life I've been touring and performing. It's what I do. But the doctors insist I stay put for awhile, so I'll heed their advice."[78]

Charles's desire to keep making music remained strong, however, and he refused to retire entirely. He was determined to keep going as long as he possibly could. At one point he commented, "If I didn't know how old I was, I'd think I was in my mid-thirties. Music to me is my blood, it's my breathing, it's my everything. . . . And I'm going to do it until God himself says, 'Brother Ray, you've been a good horse, but now I'm going to put you out to pasture.'"[79]

Two Last Projects

Although he could no longer tour, Charles remained closely involved with two high-profile projects during what proved to be his final year. One was *Ray*, a feature film based on his own life. The singer gave his personal blessing to the movie's screenwriters, James L. White and Taylor Hackford; to its director, Hackford; and to its star, Jamie Foxx. Charles followed the production of the film closely and recorded some original music for its

Actor Jamie Foxx performs as Ray Charles in a scene from *Ray*. Charles was closely involved with the production of the Oscar-winning film.

soundtrack, in particular for scenes where Foxx, as a young Ray Charles, was seen composing at the piano.

Charles was able to immerse himself almost completely in the other project. This was *Genius Loves Company*, an album of duets with an all-star cast of singers including Willie Nelson, Norah Jones, Elton John, Johnny Mathis, B.B. King, Van Morrison, Bonnie Raitt, and James Taylor. Charles was frail during its production but remained an inspiration, Raitt recalls:

He was in poor health when we did the project, and his energy was limited. But he was still sharp as a tack. He was very kind and generous and appreciative—very present. And when I heard that voice and that piano coming out of the headphones, well, that was [the] pinnacle of my career. . . . I [have] sung with some amazing people, but that was truly chilling. My only regret is that he didn't live to see how this record was received.[80]

The End of a Life

The singer's final public appearance was on April 30, 2004, at a ceremony marking the dedication of his music studio, RPM International, as one of Los Angeles's historic landmarks. Six weeks later, on June 10, surrounded by family and friends at his home, Ray Charles died of chronic liver disease. He was seventy-three.

His passing was front-page news around the world, and the tributes to his musical genius poured in from everywhere. Typical of this praise was a comment by Taylor Hackford, who had

Legendary blues guitarist B.B. King performs at Ray Charles's funeral in June 2004.

directed the movie *Ray:* "Ray Charles was definitely one of a kind. He was the best of what America is, and it was impossible not to be inspired by him."[81]

A memorial service was held for the singer on June 18, 2004, at the First African Methodist Episcopal Church in Los Angeles. Charles's body lay in an open casket, lovingly dressed in one of his trademark tuxedos. Another Charles trademark—a brand-new pair of Ray-Ban sunglasses—covered his eyes.

The service was attended by more than 1,500 invited guests— a wide range of friends, admirers, family members, politicians, actors, and musicians representing Charles's broad artistic and social appeal. Among the speakers were actors Clint Eastwood and Cicely Tyson and civil rights activists and politicians Julian Bond and the Reverend Jesse Jackson. Typical of their remarks were these words of Tyson's: "There will never be another. Through his darkness, he enlightened and brightened our lives."[82]

"Thank God for Giving Us Ray Charles"

Charles's memorial service featured several heartfelt musical tributes. Former Raelet Susaye Greene, for example, sang "The Lord's Prayer." Charles's longtime saxophonist, David "Fathead" Newman, performed the classic gospel song "Precious Lord." And Charles's friend Willie Nelson sang "Georgia on My Mind." Other performers included bluesman B.B. King, country star Glen Campbell, jazz trumpeter Wynton Marsalis, and singer Stevie Wonder.

Hundreds of mourners who could not attend personally sent floral or written tributes. Former president Bill Clinton and actor-comedian Bill Cosby both sent letters read aloud by Joe Adams. The grieving musicians and admirers included the Rolling Stones, Ice Cube, Van Morrison, the Oak Ridge Boys, and Quincy Jones. Jones, one of Charles's oldest friends, was in Russia at the time and could not get back for the service. In his place, he requested that the program include a recording with special meaning: Charles's version of the standard "My Buddy."

The Reverend Robert Robinson Sr., one of Ray Charles's twelve children, delivered a touching message during the service. Alluding to one of his father's most famous songs, the minister told the

Singer Mary J. Blige performs at a Ray Charles tribute in October 2004. In the months following Charles's death, many different musicians staged tributes to the musical legend.

assembled group, "It may be 'Crying Time,' but clap your hands, stamp your feet, stand and give God praise! Thank God for giving us Ray Charles."[83]

Remembering Brother Ray

Public praise and honors for Ray Charles continued to pour forth long after he was laid to rest in Inglewood Park Cemetery in Los Angeles. *Ray*, the film based on the singer's life, had been released just before his death. Amplified by the outpouring of public sentiment for Charles, it received tremendous acclaim and won a number of awards. These included an Oscar for Jamie Foxx's brilliant, career-making performance.

Meanwhile, Charles's last recording, *Genius Loves Company*, was released (as originally scheduled) about two months after his death. Like the movie, it was excellent in its own right but rode a huge wave of sentiment to remarkable sales and critical success. The 2005 Grammy Awards ceremony was dedicated to Charles and *Genius Loves Company* garnered eight awards there, including album of the year and record of the year (for Charles's duet with Norah Jones, "Here We Go Again").

Further memorials are in the works. Some are whimsical, such as a half-serious movement to put the singer's likeness on U.S. currency—a signal honor for a great American. Ahmir Thompson, the drummer for the band the Roots, spoke for many when he commented, "Put Ray Charles on a ten-dollar bill, that's what I say."[84] The *New Yorker* magazine published a cover showing what this might look like, with Charles's famous smile and sunglasses adorning a ten-spot.

More serious is a plan for expanding the RPM International building, already an official Los Angeles historic landmark, into a museum. This facility, being planned by Charles's business manager Joe Adams and others, will feature exhibitions spotlighting the singer's career. Ray Charles Enterprises, which continues to produce reissues of the singer's albums and create other projects, will keep its offices there.

"That Would Please Me Very Much"

All these memorials celebrate Ray Charles's brilliant, groundbreaking music. People loved his singing for many reasons, and still do; high among those reasons was its honesty. The singer commented on this in 1991 when he was asked what he would like his fans to take away with them. He replied, "What would please me is if people would say, 'One thing about Ray's music, it's sincere. You may not like everything he does, but it's real. It's always genuine.' If I got that kind of accolade for the rest of my career, or even after I'm dead, that would please me very much."[85] There seems to be little doubt that Charles's sincerity will be

"A Figure Skater's Precision"

———————————◼———————————

In his article "We Can't Stop Loving Him: Ray Charles, 1930–2004," writer David Gates of *Newsweek* offers this tribute to the singer:

> He was a musician of consummate taste—each funky little two-bar fill he played . . . had a distinct shape— and played his voice like the precious, responsive instrument it was. His timbre morphed from mellow and silky to grainy and raw; his moods swung from anguish to slyness to yearning to sheer erotic joy. He negotiated his twisty melodic ornaments with a figure skater's precision, and just when you thought he'd done all he could with that line, he would overdrive his voice into a final sob or a bright little yelp of transcendence.

remembered. Brother Ray was a complex, flawed human being, but he was also an American icon and a spellbinding musician who played it and sang it like he felt it. Charles's pioneering, dazzling merger of R&B with gospel helped create that sweet, passionate music called soul and introduce it to the world. By his own efforts and through his profound influence on generations of musicians who followed him, Ray Charles changed the course of American music and American popular culture.

Notes

Introduction: The Genius of Soul

1. Quoted in Karen Pride, "Simply Ray," *Chicago Defender*, October 26, 2004, reprinted on *Black America Today/Simply Ray*, www.blackamerica today.com/article.cfm?ArticleID=689.
2. Whitney Balliett, *American Singers: 27 Portraits in Song*. New York: Oxford University Press, 1988, p. 57.

Chapter 1: Early Childhood

3. Quoted in Michael Lydon, *Ray Charles: Man and Music*. New York: Riverhead, 1998, p. 10.
4. Ray Charles and David Ritz, *Brother Ray*. New York: Da Capo, 2003, p. 29.
5. Quoted in Balliett, *American Singers*, p. 63.
6. Quoted in Lydon, *Ray Charles*, p. 8.
7. Charles and Ritz, *Brother Ray*, p. 8.
8. Quoted in Balliett, *American Singers*, p. 64.
9. Charles and Ritz, *Brother Ray*, p. 292.
10. Quoted in Balliett, *American Singers*, p. 62.
11. Quoted in Ben Fong-Torres, "The Rolling Stone Interview: Ray Charles," *Rolling Stone*, January 18, 1973.
12. Quoted in Christopher John Farley, "Mess Around: The Genius of Ray Charles," *Time*, June 21, 2004, n.p.
13. Quoted in Balliett, *American Singers*, 1988, pp. 61–62.
14. Charles and Ritz, *Brother Ray*, pp. 24–25.

Chapter 2: The School of the Road

15. Charles and Ritz, *Brother Ray*, p. 24.
16. Charles and Ritz, *Brother Ray*, pp. 35–36.
17. Quoted in Thomas Thompson, "Music Soaring in a Darkened World," *Life*, July 29, 1966, p. 61.
18. Quoted in Farley, "Mess Around," n.p.
19. Charles and Ritz, *Brother Ray*, p. 48.
20. Lydon, *Ray Charles*, p. 21.
21. Quoted in Balliett, *American Singers*, p. 64.
22. Quoted in Balliett, *American Singers*, p. 64.
23. Charles and Ritz, *Brother Ray*, p. 58.
24. Quoted in Thompson, "Music Soaring in a Darkened World," p. 61.
25. Quoted in Lydon, *Ray Charles*, p. 25.
26. Quoted in Balliett, *American Singers*, p. 64.
27. Quoted in Guy Martin, "Blue Genius," *Esquire*, May 1986, p. 98.
28. Charles and Ritz, *Brother Ray*, p. 80.
29. Quoted in Lydon, *Ray Charles*, p. 34.
30. Charles and Ritz, *Brother Ray*, p. 73.

31. Quoted in Balliett, *American Singers*, p. 65.
32. Charles and Ritz, *Brother Ray*, p. 78.
33. Quoted in Balliett, *American Singers*, p. 65.
34. Quoted in Paul de Barros, *Jackson Street After Hours: The Roots of Jazz in Seattle*. Seattle: Sasquatch, 1993, p. 150.

Chapter 3:
From Obscurity to Stardom

35. Quoted in Lydon, *Ray Charles*, p. 54.
36. Quoted in de Barros, *Jackson Street After Hours*, p. 150.
37. Quoted in de Barros, *Jackson Street After Hours*, p. 154.
38. Quoted in Lydon, *Ray Charles*, p. 59.
39. Quoted in Lydon, *Ray Charles*, p. 76.
40. Quoted in Lydon, *Ray Charles*, p. 73.
41. Quoted in Lydon, *Ray Charles*, p. 90.
42. Quoted in Lydon, *Ray Charles*, p. 104.
43. Jerry Wexler, *Rhythm and the Blues: A Life in American Music*. New York: Knopf, 1993, p. 106.
44. Wexler, *Rhythm and the Blues*, p. 103.
45. Quoted in Lydon, *Ray Charles*, p. 128.
46. Quoted in Balliett, *American Singers*, p. 68.
47. Charles and Ritz, *Brother Ray*, p. 148.
48. Quoted in Lydon, *Ray Charles*, p. 113.
49. Quoted in Lydon, *Ray Charles*, p. 128.
50. Charles and Ritz, *Brother Ray*, p. 149.

Chapter 4: The Genius

51. Quoted in Lydon, *Ray Charles*, p. 172.
52. Richard Sudhalter, *Stardust Melody: The Life and Music of Hoagy Carmichael*. New York: Oxford University Press, 2002, p. 304.
53. Charlie Gillett, *The Sound of the City: The Rise of Rock and Roll*. New York: Pantheon, 1983, p. 202.
54. Lydon, *Ray Charles*, p. 164.
55. Quoted in Lydon, *Ray Charles*, p. 169.
56. Wexler, *Rhythm and the Blues*, p. 150.
57. Martin, "Blue Genius," p. 100.
58. Quoted in Martin, "Blue Genius," p. 96.
59. Quoted in Lydon, *Ray Charles*, p. 204.
60. Martin, "Blue Genius," p. 95.
61. Thompson, "Music Soaring in a Darkened World," p. 56.
62. Quoted in *Rolling Stone*, "Remembering Ray," July 8–22, 2004, n.p.
63. Quoted in Lydon, *Ray Charles*, p. 197.
64. Quoted in Lydon, *Ray Charles*, p. 215.

Chapter 5:
A Rough Patch for the Genius

65. Wexler, *Rhythm and the Blues*, p. 108.
66. Quoted in Lydon, *Ray Charles*, p. 255.
67. Quoted in Thompson, "Music Soaring in a Darkened World," p. 58.
68. Quoted in Lydon, *Ray Charles*, p. 257.
69. Quoted in Jon Pareles and Bernard Weinraub, "Ray Charles, Bluesy Essence of Soul, Is Dead at 73," *New York Times*, June 11, 2004.
70. Henry Pleasants, The *Great American Popular Singers*. New York: Simon & Schuster, 1974, p. 251.
71. Gillett, *The Sound of the City*, p. 203.
72. Martin, "Blue Genius," pp. 96–98.
73. Quoted in Lydon, *Ray Charles*, p. 109.
74. Charles and Ritz, *Brother Ray*, p. 160.

Chapter Six:
The Elder Statesman of Soul

75. Quoted in Lydon, *Ray Charles*, p. 343.

76. Quote in Lydon, *Ray Charles*, p. 370.

77. Quoted in *Rolling Stone*, "Remembering Ray," n.p.

78. Quoted in *Jet*, "Ray Charles: Music Legend 1930–2004," June 28, 2004, reprinted on www.findarticles.com/p/articles/mi_m1355/is_26_105/ai_n6160475.

79. Quoted in Lydon, *Ray Charles*, p. 374.

80. Quoted in *Rolling Stone*, "Remembering Ray," n.p.

81. Taylor Hackford, "Unchain My Heart," in Taylor Hackford, Jamie Foxx, James L. White, et al., *Ray: A Tribute to the Movie, the Music, and the Man.* New York: Newmarket, 2004, p. 10.

82. Quoted in Joal Ryan, "Ray Charles Goes Out in Style," on *Ray Charles News on Yahoo! Music*, http://music.yahoo.com/read/news/12177139.

83. Quoted in Hackford, "Unchain My Heart," in Hackford, Foxx, White, et al., *Ray*, p. 204.

84. Quoted in *Rolling Stone*, "Remembering Ray," n.p.

85. Quoted in Anthony DeCurtis, "Ray Charles," *Rolling Stone*, July 8–22, 2004.

For Further Reading

Books

Taylor Hackford, Jamie Foxx, James L. White, et al., *Ray: A Tribute to the Movie, the Music, and the Man.* New York: Newmarket, 2004. This large-format, generously illustrated book includes the screenplay of the feature film *Ray* and brief commentary by director Hackford and star Foxx.

David Ritz, *Ray Charles: Voice of Soul.* Philadelphia: Chelsea House, 1994. This book, part of a series called Lives of the Physically Challenged, focuses in particular on how its subject coped with blindness. It was written by the coauthor of Ray Charles's autobiography.

DVDs

O Genio: Ray Charles Live in Brazil 1963. The camera work is extremely crude by today's standards, but this mesmerizing concert footage catches Charles and his big band at the peak of their powers.

Ray. Directed by Taylor Hackford. Universal Studios, 2005. A striking, Oscar-winning performance by Jamie Foxx is the highlight of this 2004 biographical feature film.

Web Sites

RayCharles.com: The Official Site (www.raycharles.com). This extensive site, maintained by the Ray Charles Foundation, has biographical material, a discography, dedications from fans, and much more.

"Ray Charles," on Wilson & Alroy's Record Reviews (www.warr.org/charles.html). This site has capsule reviews of many of Charles's recordings, from the essential to the forgettable.

NPR: Ray Charles Dies at 73 (www.npr.org./templates/story/story.php?storyId=1953195). Viewers can listen to an audio transcript of a touching remembrance of Ray Charles by National Public Radio's Felix Contreras.

Works Consulted

Books

Whitney Balliett, *American Singers: 27 Portraits in Song.* New York: Oxford University Press, 1988. This volume of profiles by the longtime *New Yorker* jazz writer includes "It's Detestable When You Live It," a profile of Ray Charles.

Ray Charles and David Ritz, *Brother Ray.* New York: Da Capo, 2003. An updated version of Charles's 1978 autobiography, cowritten with music journalist Ritz.

Paul de Barros, *Jackson Street After Hours: The Roots of Jazz in Seattle.* Seattle: Sasquatch, 1993. This book details the history of jazz in Seattle, including the lively post–World War II scene that included Ray Charles.

Gary Giddins, *Rhythm-a-Ning: Jazz Tradition and Innovation in the '80s.* New York: Oxford University Press, 1985. A book on trends in jazz by a distinguished writer; it briefly mentions Charles.

Charlie Gillett, *The Sound of the City: The Rise of Rock and Roll.* New York: Pantheon, 1983. This is a classic, detailed text by a historian of popular music.

Michael Lydon, *Ray Charles: Man and Music.* New York: Riverhead, 1998. The only full-length biography to date of the singer, this is a detailed book by a writer for *Rolling Stone* magazine.

Henry Pleasants, *The Great American Popular Singers.* New York: Simon & Schuster, 1974. This book by a music critic contains a chapter on Ray Charles.

Richard Sudhalter, *Stardust Melody: The Life and Music of Hoagy Carmichael.* New York: Oxford University Press, 2002. This biography of the famous songwriter and performer briefly describes Ray Charles and his recording of and association with the Carmichael tune "Georgia on My Mind."

Jerry Wexler, *Rhythm and the Blues: A Life in American Music.* New York: Knopf, 1993. This memoir is by the longtime producer for Atlantic Records.

Periodicals

Anthony DeCurtis, "Ray Charles," *Rolling Stone*, July 8–22, 2004.

Christopher John Farley, "Mess Around: The Genius of Ray Charles," *Time*, June 21, 2004.

Ben Fong-Torres, "The Rolling Stone Interview: Ray Charles," *Rolling Stone*, January 18, 1973.

David Gates, "We Can't Stop Loving Him: Ray Charles, 1930–2004," *Newsweek*, June 21, 2004.

Jet, "Ray Charles: Music Legend 1930–2004," June 28, 2004, reprinted on www.findarticles.com/p/articles/mi_m1355/is_26_105/ai_n6160475.

Michael Lydon, "Raw Truth and Joy," *Atlantic Monthly*, March 1991.

Guy Martin, "Blue Genius," *Esquire*, May 1986.

Quoted in Jon Pareles and Bernard Weinraub, "Ray Charles, Bluesy Essence of Soul, Is Dead at 73," *New York Times*, June 11, 2004.

Quoted in Karen Pride, "Simply Ray," *Chicago Defender*, October 26, 2004, reprinted on *Black America Today/*

Simply Ray, www.blackamericatoday.com/article.cfm?ArticleID=689.

Bill Quinn, "The Playboy Interview: Ray Charles," *Playboy*, March 1970.

Rolling Stone, "Remembering Ray," July 8–22, 2004.

Thomas Thompson, "Music Soaring in a Darkened World," *Life*, July 29, 1966.

Internet Sources
Joal Ryan, "Ray Charles Goes Out in Style," on *Ray Charles News on Yahoo! Music*, http://music.yahoo.com/read/news/12177139.

Index

ABC-Paramount Records, 61–62
Abramson, Herb, 50
Adams, Joe, 66–67, 70, 76, 77
airplanes, 65
album sales, 82–83, 90
alto sax, 38
American Singers (Balliett), 10, 34, 40, 78
"America the Beautiful" (song), 81, 82
appearance, 40
arrangements, musical, 36, 38
arrests, 72–74
Atlantic Records, 48–50, 59, 61, 82
awards, 62, 92–94, 99

"Baby Grand" (song), 90
Balliett, Whitney, 8, 10, 34, 40, 78
band, first, 53–54
band members
  pay of, 56–57
  treatment of, 70
Basie, Count, 18
Beatles, 77–78
bepop, 35
big bands, 18, 27, 35
blindness, 19–21
blues
  blending of gospel and, 9, 43, 60, 80
  see also rhythm & blues (R&B) music
Blues Brothers, The (film), 89–90
boogie-woogie, 16
Bradley, Tom, 77
Braille, 23
Braille music notation, 27, 36, 38
Brantley, Charlie, 39
British Invasion, 77–78
Brother Ray (Charles), 20, 31, 60
Brown, Charles, 35, 36
Brown, James, 90

Brown, Ruth, 52, 53
Burnett, Carol, 70
business investments, 67
business skills, 11

Cage, Ruth, 54
call-and-response technique, 54, 59
cameo appearances, 89–90
Carter, Betty, 64
Catlett, Buddy, 43
CBS Records, 91
Cecil Shaw Singers, 51–52
charitable donations, 94
Charles, Della, 51–53, 85–86
Charles, Ray
  accomplishments of, 9–11
  determination of, 11
  development of musical style by,
    49–51, 60
  fame of, 8
  importance of music to, 11–12, 19, 20
  musical innovations of, 9–11
  obstacles overcome by, 9, 11
cheapness, 56–57, 70
chess, 76
childhood
  exposure to music during, 16, 18
  family life during, 13–16
  at Florida D&B, 21–28
  mischief during, 24
  tragedies in, 18–20
children, 85
civil rights movement, 11, 68
clarinet, 27
classical music, 27
Cole, Nat "King," 35, 37
colored musicians union, 32
comeback, 79–80

Come Live with Me (album), 82
concert tours
    declining popularity of, 87
    difficulties of, 46–49
    after drug problems, 77
    European, 67–68
    segregation and, 68
    during seventies, 83–85
    with symphonies, 88–89
"Confession Blues" (song), 38, 45
Cookies, 54–55
country music, 11, 39, 63, 68–70, 91–92
Crawford, Hank, 58
Crossover, 82
crossover hits, 59
Crying Time (album), 79–81

death, 96–97
Dedicated to You (album), 63
divorce, 85–86
Do I Ever Cross Your Mind? (album), 91
Domino, Fats, 54
donations, 94
Dowd, Tom, 59
Down Beat Records, 45
Downing, Alvin, 35
drug addiction, 45, 72–78

electric piano, 56
Ellington, Duke, 12, 18
Ertegun, Ahmet, 50, 51, 53–54, 82
European tours, 67–68
"Every Day I Have the Blues" (song), 46

family, 13–16
Feller, Sid, 70, 88
female backup singers, 54–55
film cameos, 89–90
Fisher, Mary Ann, 54
Florida Playboys, 39
Florida School for the Deaf & Blind, 21–23
    departure from, 30–31
    first year at, 23–25
    music lessons at, 26–27
    vacations from, 28–30

Fong-Torres, Ben, 63
Franklin, Aretha, 82, 89–90
Friendship (album), 92
From the Pages of My Mind (album), 91
frugality, 56–57, 70
Fulson, Lowell, 46, 49
funeral, 97–98

Garred, Milton, 42
Gates, David, 100
Genius + Soul = Jazz (album), 63
Genius Hits the Road, The (album), 62
Genius Loves Company (album), 95, 99
"Georgia on My Mind" (song), 62
Gershwin, George, 82
Gibson, Don, 71
Gillett, Charlie, 59, 82
gospel music, 9, 43, 60, 80
Grammy awards, 62, 90, 99
Grand Ole Opry, The (radio show), 18
Great Depression, 13
Greene, Susaye, 97
Greenville, Florida, 13, 14
Guitar Slim, 50

Hacker, Frederick, 76
Hackford, Taylor, 96–97
health problems, 94
hearing abilities, 32, 34
Henderson, Fletcher, 18
Hendricks, Margie, 54
heroin use, 45, 72–78
hits, 54, 59
    see also specific songs
"Hit the Road, Jack" (song), 65
Holiday, Billie, 45
Honeydrippers, 39
honorary doctorates, 93–94
honors, 92–94
hospital stay, 74–76
Howard, Della Beatrice. See Charles, Della
Hubert, Traff, 43

"I Can't Stop Loving You" (song), 71
"I Got a Woman" (song), 54

"I'll Be Good to You" (song), 90
independence, 11, 21, 25, 31, 34
"It Shoulda Been Me" (song), 50

Jacksonville, Florida, 31–35
jam sessions, 32, 34
jazz, 27
Jellyroll, 13
Joel, Billy, 90
Jones, Eddie Lee, 50
Jones, Melody, 43
Jones, Quincy, 43, 44, 90, 97
jukeboxes, 18

Kennedy Center Honor, 93

Laine, Cleo, 82
Las Vegas casinos, 87
Lauderdale, Jack, 45, 49
legacy, 93, 99–100
legal difficulties, 72–74
Levy, Joe, 80
Live at the Fillmore (album), 82
liver problems, 94
Los Angeles, 45–46
love affairs, 46, 85–86
Lydon, Michael, 30, 56, 59, 81

Mamas and the Papas, 78
Manuel's Tap Room, 35
Manzy Harris Quartet, 39
marriages, 47, 53
Martin, Guy, 19, 62, 66, 83, 84
Mayfield, Percy, 65
McCartney, Paul, 78
McKee, Garcia "Gossie", 39, 41, 42, 45
McSon Trio, 42–43, 45
memorials, 99
memorial service, 97–98
Millinder, Lucky, 39
Modern Sounds in Country and Western
  Music (album), 69–71
money, frugality with, 56–57, 70
Motown Records, 80
Mr. Pit's Red Wing Café, 16, 18

musical style
  development of, 49–51, 60
  mainstream, 62–64
  synthesis of, 9–11, 60, 80
music career
  beginnings of, 32–41
  comeback, 79–80
  during eighties and nineties,
    87–95
  first recordings, 45
  during seventies, 80–85
  as solo act, 49–51
  stardom, 58–71
  success in, 54–57
music lessons
  at Florida D&B, 26–27
  at Mr. Pit's, 18
music scene, changes in, 77–82
"My Baby" (song), 62
Myers, Larry, 61

National Medal of Arts, 93
Nelson, Willie, 92, 97
Newman, David "Fathead," 68

on-stage presence, 40, 83–85
orchestral gigs, 88–89
Orlando, Florida, 36, 38

Parker, Charlie, 44, 45
Pepsi ads, 89
performing style, 40, 83–85
Perry, Alexander, 35
personal problems
  divorce, 85–86
  drug addiction, 72–77
physical appearance, 40
piano lessons, 18, 27
Pitman, Wiley, 16
Playboys, 39
Porgy and Bess (folk opera), 82
poverty, 13
preperformance rituals, 83
Presley, Elvis, 55, 57
public image, 77

R&B music. *See* rhythm & blues (R&B) music
racial segregation, 11, 46, 68–69
radio, 18, 27
Raelets, 54–55
Raitt, Bonnie, 8, 95
Ray (film), 94–95, 98–99
Ray Charles and Betty Carter (album), 63
Ray Charles: Man and Music (Lydon), 56, 81
Ray Charles Orchestra, 11, 65, 83
record sales, 82–83, 90
Redmond, Paul J., 76
Rhythm and the Blues: A Life in American Music (Wexler), 48
rhythm & blues (R&B) music, 35–36
Richard, Keith, 91
Riddick, Gertrude, 14
Robinson, Aretha (mother), 13–16
　death of, 30–31
　　Florida D&B and, 22–23
　　self-reliance taught by, 20–21, 25
Robinson, Bailey (father), 14–15, 39
Robinson, George (brother), 15–16, 19
Robinson, Margaret, 14
Robinson, Mary Jane, 14, 15, 22
Robinson, Robert, Sr. (son), 97–98
Rock and Roll Hall of Fame, 93
rock and roll music, 77–78
RPM International, 65–67, 96, 99
Rubin, Ethel, 67

Scott, Little Jimmy, 65
Seattle, Washington, 41, 42–45
segregation, 69–69
self-reliance, 11, 21, 25, 31, 34
Shaw, Artie, 27, 29
Shaw, Cecil, 51–52
Shaw Agency, 46, 61
Sherrill, Billy, 92
Sinatra, Frank, 58
singing voice, 9, 10, 28, 50
Skyhaven Club, 39
Smith, Lawyer, 29–30
songwriting royalties, 55
soul music, 9–10, 80

Spy Hard (film), 89
Standifer, Floyd, 45
stardom, 58–71
Sudhalter, Richard, 58–59
Sullivan, Ed, 73–74
"Sun's Gonna Shine Again, The" (song), 49, 50
Sunshine Club, 36, 38
"Swanee" (song), 57
Swingtime, 49
symphony appearances, 88–89

Tallahassee, Florida, 28–30
Tampa, Florida, 39
Tampa Red, 18
Tangerine, 65
Tatum, Art, 27, 28
teenage years, 28–41
television cameos, 89–90
"This Little Girl of Mine" (song), 54
Thompson, Ahmir, 99
Thompson, Fred, 32
Thompson, Lena Mae, 32
Thompson, Thomas, 9, 34, 67–68
touring. *See* concert tours
Troupe, Vernon, 77
True to Life (Charles), 82
Turentine, Stanley, 46
Turner, Big Joe, 18
Two Spot Club, 35
Tynan, John, 64
Tyson, Cicely, 97

vocal talents, 9, 10, 28, 40

Washington, Henry, 35
"We Are the World" (benefit recording), 90
Wexler, Jerry, 48, 50, 51, 53–54, 62
"What'd I Say" (song), 59, 80
Williams, Aretha. *See* Robinson, Aretha
Williams, Eileen, 47
Wilson, Flip, 8
Wish You Were Here Tonight (album), 91

York, Tiny, 36

Picture Credits

Cover: © Tim Mosenfelder/CORBIS
Associated Press/AP, 47, 66, 73, 84
Associated Press/AP/Reuter's Pool, 81
© Bettmann/CORBIS, 14, 29, 33, 37
© CORBIS, 22
© Pierre Fournier/CORBIS, 43
© Nicola Goode/Universal Pictures/ZUMA/CORBIS, 17, 95
© Jean Guichard/SYGMA/CORBIS, 69
© Craig Lovell/CORBIS, 64
© Gerard Molina/Reuter's Pool/CORBIS, 96
© Fred Prouser/Reuters/CORBIS, 5, 8, 13, 26, 42, 58, 72, 87, 98
© Reuters/CORBIS, 88
© Ted Williams/CORBIS, 40
Hulton Archive/Getty Images, 28, 38, 48, 52, 55, 60, 79
Time-Life Pictures/Getty Images, 75. 85
Photofest, 92

About the Author

Adam Woog has written over forty books for adults, teens, and children. For Lucent Books, he has explored such subjects as Louis Armstrong, Anne Frank, Elvis Presley, sweatshops, Prohibition, and the New Deal. Woog lives with his wife and their daughter in Seattle, Washington.